7 Steps to Creating Success with Lucky Numbers

-

Jaya Karamchandani

"If you get, GIVE…
If you learn, TEACH"

–Maya Angelou

CONTENTS

About this book

Foreword

Few Myth Busters

Dedication

Introduction
    What is your Number?
    HOW DOES DAY NUMBER AND POWER NUMBER HELP?
    NUMBERS AND THE RULING PLANETS
    NUMBERS AND THE ZODIAC SIGNS
    HOW DOES NAME NUMBER HELP?
    KNOW YOUR PERSONAL YEAR AND PERSONAL DAY
    SOLUTIONS

About the Author

Meaning of the power numbers

Chapter 1 - All about **Number 1**
    All those born on 1st, 10th, 19th and 28th of any given month

Chapter 2 - All about **Number 2**
    All those born on 2nd, 11th, 20th and 29th of any given month

Chapter 3 - All about **Number 3**
    All those born on 3rd, 12th, 21st and 30th of any given month

Chapter 4 - All about **Number 4**
    All those born on 4th, 13th, 22nd and 31st of any given month

Chapter 5 - All about **Number 5**
    All those born on 5th, 14th and 23rd of any given month

Chapter 6 - All about **Number 6**

All those born on 6th, 15th and 24th of any given month

Chapter 7 - All about Number 7
All those born on 7th, 16th and 25th of any given month

Chapter 8 - All about Number 8
All those born on 8th, 17th and 26th of any given month

Chapter 9 - All about Number 9
All those born on 9th, 18th and 27th of any given month

Conclusion

ABOUT THIS BOOK

All rights including copyrights, publication, translations, etc., are reserved with the author only. No part of this book may be reproduced or transmitted in any form or by any means, electronic, mechanical, photocopying, recording or otherwise, or stored in any form whatsoever.

© Jaya MK
© Jaya Karamchandani
Email-jayamk@invinciblepassiontalkshow.com
Web address- http://www.invinciblepassiontalkshow.com/about-us/

Disclaimer - The views and insights expressed in this book are the personal views of the author. Publisher/Author will not be liable for any direct, indirect, consequential, or incidental damages arising out of use (direct or indirect) of the book or its solutions or recommendations. Due care and diligence have been exercised while editing this book. However, neither author nor the publisher or editor holds any responsibility for any mistake or omission that may have inadvertently taken place. All legal issues are subject to the State of Georgia, Forsyth County jurisdiction only.

Foreword

"7 STEPS TO CREATING SUCCESS WITH LUCKY NUMBERS"

Years back I noticed the recurrence of some numbers and then a pattern of events. The curiosity to see if there is a connection and what is the meaning of those numbers, the clues, the signs and the message that the Universe was trying to relay, made me a number influencer of this predictive science called "NUMEROLOGY".

With every research and study, one thing was clear that numbers are more magical than you can imagine. Just like the presence of electricity leads to light but no one has seen electricity, similarly the good and bad events in life are seen, not the force behind it.

Understanding numbers can lead you to understand how they work, just like knowing how electricity works. Once you know that, you can produce electricity and put to great use.

My biggest frustration was not finding books which did exactly that. So, I took the advice of the late Maya Angelou's saying, "IF YOU GET, **GIVE.** IF YOU LEARN, **TEACH**".

This book will help you learn and use this knowledge in 7 Steps.

This book is the result of my years of research, experience, and practice of Numbers. (You see numbers everywhere. Be it in your phone numbers, house number, bank account number and age number.)

This book will walk you through numbers of your date of birth and how it has the secret code to solving the puzzle called DESTINY. Each one of you has your unique IP - your numbers, and the key to having success in life lies in your unique numbers.

If you are reading this book, then I believe you are either interested in knowing more about this 5000-year-old predictive science called "numerology" or would like to know "how to use numbers to have success in life."

This book will give you answers to all. Stay with me so that, at the end of the book, you can decode the meaning of your numbers.

This book is to guide you in your path, and the journey of (your) life, so that you can understand why you were chosen with a particular birth of date, why were you connected to certain circumstances, and why were you given a certain set of people in your life.

Your life is the perfect blend of happiness, sadness, rejection, joy, failure, success, and much more. Knowing your numbers, helps you to be prepared and guide yourself better but not to run away from it. Well, you can never run away from your destiny, or can you?

Life is a series of dots, and it is not connecting those dots that matter, but it is embracing the message sent via those dots.

<u>**Success is 70% Mindset, 20% strategy and 10% connections**</u>. This strategy is knowing how to use your connections, your skills, and where. This book is going to show you how to use your surplus gold that will bring returns beyond your dreams.

Your date of birth is the code for unlocking your surplus gold. Before you know where to invest, you should know your gold.

Each number in your date of birth holds a unique kind of surplus gold. This book will reveal to you the 7 steps to creating success with numbers. Let's begin!

Few Myth Busters

Myth - You have to be born lucky
Fact - You can create your luck

Myth - You have to work hard to succeed
Fact - You have to work smart to succeed

Myth - Success is all about hard work
Fact - Success is all about 70% Mindset, 20% Strategy, 10% Connections.

Myth -This book will change your life
Fact - This book will help you create success with numbers

Myth - You can change your destiny
Fact - You can prepare yourself to shape your destiny

DISCLAIMER: Just like the weather channel predicts about rain, hurricane, tornado, high winds and other natural happenings so you may prepare yourself better for that weather. Similarly, this book cannot change what was given to you by way of your destiny, but it can help you prepare yourself better to face it or minimize the harmful effects and maximize the beneficial results.

THESE ARE MY OPINIONS AND IDEAS, AND I DO NOT GUARANTEE ANY RESULTS.

DEDICATION

To my family and friends, who always supported me and helped me spread my wings even when it wasn't easy. I am grateful that your support and inspiration gave me the strength to make this happen.

To my husband, who gives me the reason to always give my best and to persevere. Your unconditional support and love has been the key to the creation of this book.

To my kids, who understood what I was doing and their love for constantly making this book better, especially for helping to create the cover art and editing of this book.

Also to all those people around the world who have interest in this science and want to make their lives better. If this book can help and serve you, it will be an honor. Thank you so much for being part of the Invincible Success community. I feel blessed to be able to help others gain their freedom, success, and have a better life.

Introduction

DO NOT SKIP THIS PART OF THE BOOK

Numerology is all about the harmony of numbers. This alignment is created by making slight changes in the spelling of your name, use of colors, dates to follow and the way you write your signature.

That brings great success in the areas of education, career, job, business, health, personal matters and marriage compatibility.

This section will show you about -

- What are numbers?
- What is the day number?
- What is the power number?
- How to calculate the name number?
- What are the various planetary influences of numbers?

Let me ask you this, would you take your Toyota Prius to a race track to compete with a Lamborghini and Ferrari? Most likely not. Both are cars, but each has different strengths. One is known for its efficiency, and the other for its speed. Each number has its own strength and each number shines in a different industry but you cannot expect one number to play the same strength as the other.

The key to winning is to play to your strengths.

Everyone is born on different dates, and that makes every one of you, UNIQUE. **The key is to know your strengths just like knowing the horsepower of your engine.** Do you have an efficient V4, or a powerful but gas guzzling V12? If you know your strengths and weaknesses just like the horsepower and speed, then you will never disappoint yourself.

This book will walk you through the process of understanding your strengths as well weakness from your date of birth. Then it will provide you, solutions to boost the horsepower and speed of your success.

Are you ready to create your success in 7 steps?

Each number is a vibration that shapes your life. Just like electricity makes things work but you can't see it. Similarly, number vibrations make your life great or rough even though you can't see it.

The day of your birth holds the key to your talents, your tools and your strengths and weakness. Let's say you want to bake your cake, for that you would need ingredients eg. milk, sugar, eggs, flour, and butter.

Same analogy goes with NUMBERS. **Before you decide, which business you want to start or which career path you want to choose, wouldn't be great to know what are your talents and strengths and if the chosen business or career will provide success or not?**

Find here the meaning of your day number and power number so you can put it to use and achieve success.

1. WHAT IS YOUR NUMBER?

Everyone has few numbers on their back. These are your birth numbers. Each number is a vibration that shapes your life. Just like electricity makes things work but you can't see it. Number is an energy that shapes your life but you cannot see it.

However, you can use this number energy to make things work out for you by understanding these rules.

Find here the meaning of day numbers, so you know about your talents and strengths and where you can use it.

It will help you to understand the meaning of your power number, the purpose of your life, the business or career where you will achieve success.

NUMERICAL VALUES OF EACH ALPHABET

Let's first understand the numbers. Numerology is about 5000-year-old predictive science, and it guides you through your life. I practice the **Chaldean Numerolog**y. There are few basic number vibrations that exist in everyone's life. These are from numbers 1 through 9. Every alphabet has a numerical value attached. Here is the chart below:

1	2	3	4	5	6	7	8
A	B	C	D	E	U	O	F
I	K	G	M	H	V	Z	P

J	R	L	T	N	W		
Q		S		X			
Y							

Now for you to find the name number for JOHN MYERS, calculate the value like this:

J	O	H	N		M	Y	E	R	S
1	7	5	5		4	1	5	2	3

Next, add all the numbers- 1+7+5+5+4+1+5+2+3=33/6
Name adds to 33/6

Suppose the birth date is -
Date of birth – April 23, 1965
His day number is 23. Add both digits, and you get 2+3=5
For his destiny/power number, add all the numbers, and you get 4+2+3+1+9+6+5=30/3

Let's see few more examples. You have to calculate the name number that you are mostly known by. **However, you should use the name that is most fortunate for you and helps you thrive.

Let us take the example of the famous and successful American media proprietor, talk show host, actress, producer, and philanthropist. She is most known for her highest-rated television show of its kind in the history and stayed as number one show for almost 25 years, "The Oprah Winfrey Show."

Oprah Winfrey's -

Her date of birth- January 29, 1954 (1.29.1964)
Day number – 29/11/2
Life path/Destiny/Power number – 13/4

OPRAH GAIL WINFREY
23   8   28   =   59/5

OPRAH WINFREY

23 28 = 51/6

Please refer to the meaning of number 59/5 as well as 51/6 in the relevant number 5 and number 6 chapter.

Please remember there are very successful personalities who by destiny acquired a lucky name number. But there are few who even though with the backing of lucky day and power numbers, have not been able to achieve success due to unlucky name number.

To achieve the full potential of your numbers, you have to find out which name number is most fortunate and use that in everyday life from signing documents, in social media, business name and logo.

Now let's see the example of **Martin Luther King Jr**

Date of birth – January 15, 1929 (1.15.1969)
Day number- 15/6
Destiny/Power Number – 1

Martin Luther King Jr
17   25   11   3   =   56/11/2

MLK Jr
432   12   = 12/3

NOTE - PLEASE REMEMBER IF YOU USE MRS., CPA, DR, JUNIOR, SENIOR, ETC. IN YOUR NAME THEN THAT NEEDS TO BE CALCULATED IN YOUR NAME NUMBER TOO.

**The key here is to remember that your name number will impact your life as per the date and destiny number and you will experience the influence. So, lucky or unlucky whatever numbers you received at your birth cannot be changed, but to have smooth sailing, you can change your name, signature, use of colors, use of certain days and dates, etc.

**TAKEAWAY- For businesses, if you spend money on marketing but not in naming your brand, then products will fail to live up to your expectations.

STOP! BEFORE YOU MOVE FURTHER, TRY TO FIND YOUR DAY NUMBER, POWER NUMBER, AND NAME NUMBER.

2. How does Day Number and Power Number help?

This is where the magic happens. Day number holds the key to knowing about your personality, potential, talents, strengths, weaknesses, and who you are. Just like whether you are Lamborghini, Ferrari, Porsche or Toyota Prius!

Power Number is the key to finding your life's purpose, your path, right career and business. Once you figure this thing out, then you can use your day number (that holds the key to your potential, talents, and strengths) to achieve success. Knowing your power number helps you to find out how far you can go with your talents! Just like knowing the horsepower of your car, you know the maximum speed of the car and the distance it can go.

3. Numbers and the ruling planets

The reason every number impacts your life is because every number represents a ruling planet. Each planet has its benefits and discomforts. When a particular number/planet rules your life, you experience either smooth sailing or constant challenges.

Number 1 represents Planet **SUN**
Number 2 represents Planet **MOON**
Number 3 represents Planet **JUPITER**
Number 4 represents Planet **URANUS**
Number 5 represents Planet **MERCURY**
Number 6 represents Planet **VENUS**
Number 7 represents Planet **NEPTUNE**
Number 8 represents Planet **SATURN**
Number 9 represents Planet **MARS**

4. Numbers and Zodiac Signs

Every zodiac sign has an impact on a number. So, let's say in this example, John Myers with the date of birth- April 23, 1965, with zodiac sign Aries and it's ruling planet Mars. Mars is a fiery planet, and its number is 9.

John will have the speed of fire, energy, and he might be a go-getter, short-tempered and so on. This impact is due to number 9.

Knowing your zodiac number is another piece of solving this puzzle of life called "LUCK."

5. How does Name Number help?

Name Number plays an important role in one's success. **A good name number gives power, luck, and brings success.**

Remember each name number is a planetary vibration that produces electromagnetic energy, and if it is in alignment with your lucky numbers, you will have success. If there isn't alignment, then you will experience discomfort, delay, and doubts.

Name Number 1 – Planet Sun is the ruling planet for this number. This name number is ideal for someone with interest in the business or the service industry.

Name Number 2 – Planet Moon is the ruling planet for this number. Indeed this number is often seen in the name number of people in the creative industry such as acting, music, drama, etc.

Name Number 3 – Planet Jupiter is the ruling planet for this number. A business that requires great public speaking or self-expression has this name number.

Name Number 4 – Planet Uranus is the ruling planet for this number. This number is a spiritual number and should be avoided if one desires materialistic gain and desires smooth sailing in life.

Name Number 5 – Planet Mercury is the ruling planet for this number. You would often see this number on the back of famous personalities in the public speaking industry as well as sports industry, especially in the water sports. This number is equally good for travel industry too.

Name Number 6 – Planet Venus is the ruling planet for this number. This number is often on the back of popular personalities in the entertainment and media industry. This number provides name and fame along with materialistic success.

Name Number 7 – Planet Neptune is the ruling planet for this number. This number is a double-edged sword. This name number is usually found on the back of profoundly spiritual and enlightened personalities. This number helps them to get to the top, but not everyone can handle this number. Similarly, not very many can be advised to have this name number because it brings a lot of struggles, but if success is achieved, then it stays there forever.

Name Number 8 – Planet Saturn is the ruling planet for this number. This name number does not suit everyone. In fact, it might bring more legal battles and troubles than benefits. However, if one has strong Saturn placement in the native numbers or birth chart, then it's pure gold for them.

Name Number 9 – Planet Mars is the ruling planet for this number. This name number is usually found in the people in food, construction, and real-estate industry. Some of the top celebrity chefs have this number backing. In fact, this number is the high energy packed Number, so it does suit people in the telecommunications industry too.

6. KNOW YOUR PERSONAL YEAR AND PERSONAL DAY

The personal year helps you find out about how the coming year is going to be for you, what it holds, and how you can use this information for planning. Knowing your personal year is like knowing the weather and finding out if it's going to rain or shine. If you are planning to cookout, then you need shine because you can't cookout when it's raining. Similarly, if you know how the year is going to be, you can plan accordingly.

Meaning of Personal Year
Knowing what the year has in store for you and how it's going to be, will provide a great insight and helps you prepare better. Similarly knowing how the day will go for you will help you plan.

How to calculate personal year?
Add your day and month of birth to the current year. Suppose you want to know how is this year 2017 going to be for you. If your date of birth is June 14, 1977, then -
Number 6 for the month of June, 5 for adding 14 and 1 for the year 2017.
Add 6+5+1=12/3(reduce it to single digit)
Hence this year is number 3 for you.

Find out the meaning of the personal year below:

- **Personal Year 1**: Fresh start, new projects, new ideas, planting new seed for new beginnings.
- **Personal Year 2**: Focus on building personal relationships, mutual growth for family as well professional.
- **Personal Year 3**: Time to rise and shine with all your creativity, power and inspiration.

- **Personal Year 4:** Play safe and carefully as this year is for hard work, building routine, careful approach to work and dedication to rules.
- **Personal Year 5**: Time to explore, bring your personality out, communicate, thrive and be free like a bird. Overall a year of change. Be careful and not let go of stability.
- **Personal Year 6**: Be ready to take on responsibilities personally and professionally.
- **Personal Year 7**: Lot of loneliness, feeling of an outcast, spiritual realization, separation, and self-introspection. However, do not try to make decisions of separation or divorce this year as might regret.
- **Personal Year 8:** The hard work you put brings fruits, joy, and results.
- **Personal Year 9**: Time to wrap up, let go and get ready for a new journey starting next year that transforms your life.

How to calculate personal day?

If you know what the day has in store for you, you will be surprised to see how accurate it is. Find out the meanings and how to calculate the personal day here.
Suppose your date of birth is June 14, 1977, and you want to know how your day is going to be on August 15, 2017.

Here is how you calculate:
Add your month and day of birth to current day, month and year.
This case your day of birth is 14/5 and month is 6 for June.
Next add 8 for the month of August, 6 for day 15, and 1 for the year 2017.
Now add all: 5+6+8+6+1=17/8
Therefore, August 15, 2017, is day 8 for you.

Find out the meanings of the personal day here:

- **Personal Day 1:** You have great ideas, and you are focused on your own goals but don't let others dissuade you. Go on your own, for a new start.
- **Personal Day 2:** Try to bring harmony in your personal and professional matters. Right day to sort out differences.
- **Personal Day 3:** Fun is in the air today. A time to unwind and enjoy.
- **Personal Day 4:** Try to settle business matters as it needs attention now. Time to get organized.

- **Personal Day 5**: Great day to travel, renovation, and new friendships.
- **Personal Day 6:** Matters at family or business end needs attention and need to make few important decisions.
- **Personal Day 7**: Don't engage in family discussions and don't try to settle matters as it will be disastrous. However, if you want a legal matter to be settled, then pick day 7 or break a bad partnership, today is the day!
- **Personal Day 8:** Perfect day to invest and increase your finances Go ahead to make business decisions. Time to ask for raise or promotion. Gamble.
- **Personal Day 9:** Time to let it go, care, share with others and not to worry. Don't start new business or investment or ask for any financial gain today.

Here you go! A quick way to remember basic meanings.

ONE is FUN
TWO to TANGO
THREE for FREE
FOUR to GROW
FIVE to FLY
SIX go FIX
SEVEN not FINE
EIGHT gets RATE
NINE go DINE

7. SOLUTIONS

Now you cannot change your date of birth numbers and its impact on your life. But that doesn't mean you have to struggle all through your life. Not only the numbers guide you about your right career, business, relationship, partnership, friends, and health but also provide you simple solutions.

Follow along to find out how you can create your success in 7 Steps!!!

About the Author

Jaya Karamchandani is a proud mother, wife, author, founder & host of the "Invincible Passion Talkshow." (http://www.invinciblepassiontalkshow.com/about-us/). An Indian-American with a double Bachelors', Masters' degree and a foreign attorney, she enjoys wearing a variety of professional hats.

She always had interest and curiosity to find out the reasons for believing anything to be true. This curiosity led her to explore the mystery behind recurrence of some numbers again and again in her life. This led her to study numerology and the key to unlocking the mindset power. She calls it "Transpirational Approach."

If you want to learn and understand how this science of numbers can help you transform your life, do subscribe to her channel – InvinciblePassionTalkshow. YouTube:
http://www.youtube.com/c/JayaKaramchandani?sub_confirmation=1

Connect with her on the social –

Twitter: https://twitter.com/1jayamk/
Facebook: https://www.facebook.com/Jayamkaramchandani/
Instagram: https://www.instagram.com/Jayamkinvincble/
Website: https://invinciblepassiontalkshow.com/Contact
Email: invinciblepassiontalkshow@gmail.com
Pinterest: https://www.pinterest.com/JayaMKInvincble/pins/

This journey outward is only a fraction of her inner journey, something her soul longed to create and do. She got serious to find answers to her burning desire about the mysteries of struggles and success in people's lives. Her biggest question was that "Is it the coincidence that 97% people work hard at the 9-5 job and live paycheck to paycheck but 3% people enjoy the wealth?"

This CANNOT BE JUST A COINCIDENCE!!!

Her attorney mind forced to find evidence and she saw a similarity of numbers in all those who made to Fortune and Forbes list. That was also the moment that she realized that "success leaves BIG clues" and "success is duplicable."

That dream and desire lead to conclusions that "success is 70% mindset, 20% strategy and 10% connections." She started inspiring the mind of entrepreneurs with passion, why trusting the Universe helps you with your purpose and finding true calling via her weekly talk show http://www.invinciblepassiontalkshow.com/about-us/. She teaches the transpirational approach to mindset success. The inspiration that transforms your life every day. You become your teacher-preacher.

As part of 20% Strategy to creating success, then she started practicing this number science and saw excellent results and started helping her friends. She helps businesses and individuals find the industry as well career that will be most rewarding and fulfilling emotionally, financially and spiritually.

She helps you launch your brand, leverage your brand name and maximize its potential by strategizing your lucky numbers; leveraging social media networking and harnessing the mindset power.

Mindset is a gold mine, and the key to unlocking your potential lies in your numbers. If you can use it and implement as per the 7 steps, your game plan will be unbeatable. She helps you access your most significant fortune (your mindset) and use your numbers to make the world a better place for yourself and others.

If you are interested in finding out more about Jaya Karamchandani, you can get in touch with her at http://www.invinciblepassiontalkshow.com/contact/

Meaning of the power numbers

The power number is the key to finding your life purpose, path, right career or business. It is the total of all the numbers of your birth date.

Suppose your date of birth is October 28, 1955. It adds to 10+28+1955=22/4. Always reduce the number to a single digit. But the influence of inherent numbers of double-digit gives a deeper understanding of the true life purpose.

The power number in this case is 22/4.

The other number you have to keep in mind is the maturity number that comes into play after the age of 40. Maturity number is your day number and power number combined. So, in this case, the maturity number would be 28+22=50/5 (day number+power number= maturity number)

The maturity number is sometimes the second career or the turn that your life will take after 40. This is where you will settle or find your true calling. **A detailed information about the right profession or business for the numbers 1-9 can be found in the individual chapters for each number.**

Now let's find the meaning of the power numbers here-

Number 1 - The world is a better place because of number 1 leaders. Number 1 makes them a great leader, visionary, researcher and humble. Their success comes after trials and tribulations. But the feat they accomplish is not possible for any other number. This number earns wealth and respect by following the unconventional path. In fact, they create their own path and the world joins them. You can leave them, shun them or ridicule them, they will come back and become a phoenix again. **Steve Jobs and Martin Luther King Jr. had power number 1!**

Number 2 - This power number goes through many different facets of life. They rise to fame on the basis of their inner wisdom and by trusting their instinct. Procrastination is their biggest enemy. If you can get them to work in that moment of doubt, they can then move the mountains. They can be great in politics, sports, marine, arts, creative fields and technology business industry. **Barack Obama and Evan Spiegel has power number 2!**

Number 3 - This power number is a business leader. They thrive in business and often have lead roles in the administration. They see opportunities and turn them into profits. Their strong acumen and knack for business is what helps them shine and earn great name and fame. **Hillary Clinton and Lee Shau Kee has power number 3!**

Number 4 - This power number is pure gold in terms of "willpower, hard work and loyalty". If you have a friend with this number don't leave them. This number 4 is organized, dedicated and sincere number. They work very hard and turn the adversities into opportunities. Their success is the ultimate manifestation of their will-power. They are very spiritual and intuitive. They believe in divinity.
Oprah Winfrey and Bill Gates has power number 4!

Number 5 - This power number is an adventurer and a great communicator. They like to live life on their own terms and fly like a free bird. Rules and regulations suffocate them and they cannot stay in one relationship for long if it gets suffocating for them. The same is true for business. They need the passion and drive to keep them motivated. Change is the key to their happiness. They have charismatic personality and money comes to them easily. They are intelligent as well intuitive. **Michael Bloomberg and Mark Zuckerberg has power number 5**

Number 6 - This power number is responsibility and relationship. They enjoy luxuries and crave for freedom. However, this number demands support and taking responsibility. So, whatever you do, don't ignore your personal relationships. Their success comes when they find the balance between material world and personal world. The desire to be free and the need to take responsibility has to be balanced well. They do great in creative business fields and that's where they belong.
Jeff Bezos and Warren Buffett has power number 6!

Number 7 - This power number makes one researcher, introvert, curious about mystic world, highly intelligent, inquisitive and non-traditional leader. They never chase material success and like being aloof. They show up when it's the time. They are healers and preachers and they do great in the self-development industry and in writing.
Sheryl Sandberg and Taylor Swift has power number 7!

Number 8 - This power number is about success, leadership, material success, ambitions and wealth. Number 8 is the result of satisfying karmic debt and once that is paid off and lessons are learnt, the life rewards you with

success. It is a dual number of spiritual and material success. Those with Number 8 life path are brave, fighters, courageous and they don't give up. Life brings them many choices and makes it hard to get to the final destination but they make it. They usually see growth after the age of 40.
Nelson Mandela and Alexander Graham Bell had power number 8!

Number 9 - This power number craves for social upliftment. They are the torch bearers of new revolution. They sacrifice their life for the welfare of the society. They find their success by making the world a better place. Their inner wisdom makes them wise and the desire to help the society turns them into a humanitarian or a leader who serves the community by unique ways. You could be a business owner and solving the society problems by providing a solution. Ruled by 9 makes you energetic and full of fire.
Mother Teresa and Mahatma Gandhi had power number 9!

"Born on October 28, 1955 (28 adds to number 1) this young man changed the way world relates to computers. This young man with his sheer foresightedness, smart work, perseverance and entrepreneurship changed the lives of many. He has been included in the Forbes list of the world's wealthiest people since 1987 and until recently he held the title of the richest person in the world. No wonder he is number 1 born (28=1)- one of the lucky numbers"

- **Meet BILL GATES-** American business tycoon, investor, philanthropist, author and co-founder of the Microsoft.

Another example of extraordinary success of number 1 is of Amancio Ortega, born on March 28, 1936 (day 28 adds to 1)

CHAPTER 1 - ALL ABOUT NUMBER 1

Knowing your numbers is like knowing the horsepower of your car. However, there are few numbers which always seem to have an easy ride in life. These are **numbers 1,3, 5 and 6.**

Here are the examples of the few names of the TOP Youngest Billionaires of the world in 2017. It CAN'T BE A COINCIDENCE that their names add to one of the Lucky Numbers of 1,3,5, and 6!

Check it out yourself-

> Mark Zuckerberg (Facebook) - **Name Number 1**
> Lukas Walton (Wal-Mart) - Name **Number 5**
> Dustin Moskovitz (Asana) - Name **Number 1**
> Yang Huiyan (Country Garden Group) - Name **Number 11**
> Nathan Blecharczyk (Airbnb) - Name **Number 1**
> Brian Chesky (co-founder Airbnb) - Name **Number 3**

Day Number 1 –

Those born on 1st, 10th,19th and 28th of any given month are Number 1 personalities. The day number is the key to understanding your talents and strengths.

Power Number aka Life Purpose –

Those born on any date of any given month but having the power number 1 are also Number 1 personalities. It is the key to finding which business or career will bring you success.

Zodiac Ruler -

If your zodiac sign is Leo, then you are ruled by Planet Sun and number 1. Knowing the ruling planet can help you either maximize the beneficial results of your lucky number or minimize the harmful effects of unlucky number influence. This is usually done by the name change.

Name Number -

If the alphabet values in your name add to 1, then you are ruled by Number 1 too.

Characteristics -

The people under the influence of number 1 are the ones who mostly lead. Be it in any field and they are known for their leadership. Now, every number has some great strengths as well weaknesses.

Number 1 personalities always aim for high visions and goals in life. They enjoy all the riches and comforts of life, and this makes them workaholics. Their success mantra is speed, confidence, and straightforwardness. With these key strengths, they advance in life in whatever endeavor they undertake. However, this haste sometimes brings obstacles and failures due to not looking into the details.

They are very independent by nature and hold themselves in high-honor. To them their integrity and dignity is everything. They do not hesitate to help others, and they do so without expectation of any return. Their swift mind presents them with a quick analysis of any given situation, and strong intellect helps them grasp situation very easily.

Their honesty and straightforwardness do bring them many enemies, competitors, and setbacks. However, they don't stop until they achieve their goals. So, they are quick to recover from their setbacks.

Due to their high demanding nature, they do not make very many friends and the ones they make, stay with them and they take good care of their friends.

CEOs, top executives, politicians, business owners, leaders, doctors, and creative field professionals have the number 1 with them.

Each number has some negative influence on the person too. The above-mentioned qualities take place when the ruling planet - Sun has proved beneficial to the person who is under its influence. But when the Sun is not beneficial, then the person will face delay, defamation, will be lavish in their spending, and known for wrong reasons. So, when the Sun's impact is weak in their numbers, then you would see these number 1 people working in the lower level or administrative jobs.

LIGHTBULB: This is where numerology can be very helpful. If you know that you have number 1 with you and you are going through struggles, then get a consult to change that and how you can have a smooth sailing. A lot can be done to bring your name in harmony with your lucky numbers.

So how does name change help? A simple illustration will help-

Illustration - It's like if you don't have a skill that you can leverage to establish yourself as an expert, but you know how to leverage other's skills. Then you will use that to build your fortune. Same way, if you know you have number 1, then

Numerology has solutions on how you can leverage that to build your fortune and bring positive changes in your lifestyle.

Specific characteristics: Apart from this, there might be few specific characteristics as per their actual day of birth. I am giving some more insight below-

Day Number 1 –
Being a single digit number 1, they have lack of patience and want everything instantly. The habit of speaking their mind makes them sound rude but their self-confidence brings them success and so do many enemies. If they learn to speak socially and politically way, they can be the winners.

Day Number 10 –
This number 10 makes them careful, introvert and caring. Their desire for affection and validation is key to their happiness.

Day Number 19 –
Number 19 born are smart, sharp and very reserved. They don't reveal their inner feelings and outer persona might be not real. So, people find them as confused and un-trustworthy. If they manage to trust but still be careful and become flexible, they would have better sailing in life.

Day Number 28 –
Those born on 28th are smart and attractive. The ruling planet Sun is not that prominent in their lives so that can cause eyesight or health or career problems. But no worries as the solutions of using lucky days, dates and precious stones take care of that.

VARIOUS VARIATIONS OF NAME NUMBER 1 SERIES
(How to calculate name number is shown in the section "Introduction")

As mentioned previously, if the name number adds to 1 series, then you will be under the influence of Number 1 too. Below are the specific characteristics of various variations of Name Number 1.

Name Number 10 –
This number brings respect and honor. However, the presence of "0" will bring some kind of lack and so their luck will go through lot of ups and downs. The honesty will bring them stability in the latter part of their life.

Name Number 19 –
This is a very fortunate number to have. This number shows its positive results slowly and brings name, fame, and wealth. However, honesty is the key to maintaining the good luck.

Name Number 28 –
Due to the presence of 2 and 8, they face lot of struggles and hardships in the life. But they start all over again as its bigger form of "1". They achieve success and earn their wealth as well success.

Name Number 37 –
Another very lucky name number to have for those with 1. This number is often the force behind "rags-to-riches" success and gifted prodigies. However, they should practice self-restraint and loyalty in personal relationships.

Name Number 46 –
This number brings fortune and fame with the help of intelligence, knowledge power and persistence. This name number is the organic approach to success and huge success. So, the true winner of making an ordinary into an extraordinary in life, usually has this name number.

Name Number 55 –
This lucky number with backing of double "5" is a great example of intuition and self-control. They can achieve anything they want and they usually are very highly regarded in their industry. However, my experience has shown that if they have birth number of 5 in any form, then they should not have this name number. Remember too much of anything becomes a danger!

NOTE - Name number that adds to after 55 can be reduced to the next double digit number series.

Lucky Dates -
Those who have the number 1 influence either by way of the day or power number or name number, they can start using their lucky dates.

These dates are -
1,10,19, and 28

Using lucky dates increases chances of success, favorable networking, successful partnerships, and long-lasting positive results.

The other important number and friendly **dates are of number 7, 16, and 25**. Try to do your important meetings, events, deals and efforts on this day.

Friendly Dates –

The dates of 4, 13, 22 and 31 will deliver important things in your life. The changes would be beneficial as well unpredictable.

Unlucky Dates –

Dates 8th,17th, and 26th of any given month should be avoided as these will add to the misery, struggle, difficulties, and failures.

Avoid starting a new project, naming your business, or partnerships on these dates. However, number 8 by itself does not create turbulences in life. It should be viewed as a stepping stone to a better future. It's just a forewarning of the results if a new project or important things are started on number 8.

Business Relationships -
Number 1 people are very stubborn and hard to convince. They don't change their decisions easily, and they don't like being bossed! As such they are not too adaptable for business ventures. However, it would be wise to do business partnerships with people born under the influence of 4 Only. Sometimes number 7 will come to rescue.

Avoid partnerships with those under the influence of 2 and 8 at all cost as this usually results in a business loss, lack of profits and eventually closure of the venture.

Personal Relationships -

They seem to have a happy life if they marry those in number series of 3, 5 and 6. However, I do not recommend a number 1 marrying another number 1.

NOTE - No matter how great the numbers are, if the marriage date is not lucky; the results could be adverse. So, keep that in mind before selecting a date. Use your lucky dates for that purpose too.

LIGHTBULB: This is where numerology is very helpful as a number-influencer can advise on the business prospect, future of your business or career path and also which line of work/business will be fortunate based on your day, power, zodiac and name number.

Lucky Colors -
When naming your business, or designing your logo, you as a future entrepreneur or current biz owner should use your lucky colors.

Lucky colors for number 1 are shades of yellow, very light red in fact on the orange side and light blue.

Unlucky Colors -
Avoid black and brown color as it brings misfortune unless your love misery.

Precious Stones & Metal -
Gold proves lucky to them and wearing Ruby would bring positive results.

Solutions-
If you are facing health issues, use your lucky stone.
If you are facing financial issues, give something in charity on Sunday.
You can also donate every month red kidney beans, clothes or some red things to a needy or to an orphanage.
You can keep a copper coin in your wallet or purse and change it every full moon. If it helps, continue doing it.
Avoid eating meat on Sunday or dates of 1, 10, 19 and 28.
For overall benefits, meditate while holding yellow flowers in your hand and then letting flowers flow in running water of your kitchen sink. Do this every Sunday.
Wear your lucky colors on a daily basis.
Set up important meetings or interview on your lucky days or dates.
Focus on early morning rising sun for few minutes and absorb those rays. It will be beneficial.

IMPORTANT THING TO REMEMBER -
These alphabets represent number 1 as their value is 1.
A, I, J, Q, Y
So how you can use this information is by naming your business with these letters if you want a powerful dose of number 1.

Here are few references to top power names to illustrate how their success is the result of not just hard work but from the presence of lucky numbers too.

(Source- https://www.cbsnews.com/pictures/richest-people-in-world-forbes/)
(https://www.forbes.com/billionaires/list)

Examples:

Companies with Name Number 1
(source- http://fortune.com/global500/list/)

Company name	Name Number
BP	10/1
DISNEY	19/1
ROYAL DUTCH SHELL	55/1
GOOGLE	28/1

People with Name Number 1

Power Names	Name Number
JOHN MARS	28/1
MARK ZUCKERBERG	46/1
JEFF BEZOS	46/1
ROB WALTON	37/1

Now let's see how you can use this information to create your business success in 7 STEPS. I am explaining about Google here.

So, Google Founders, Larry Page and Sergey Brin founded Google on September 4,1988.

LARRY PAGE –
Date of Birth March 26,1973
Day - 8
Power Number – 4 (3+26+1973=4)
Zodiac sign - Aries (Ruler Mars, Number 9)

SERGEY BRIN –
Date of Birth August 21,1973
Day - 3
Power Number - 4 (8+21+1973=4)
Zodiac sign - Leo (Ruler Sun, Number 1)

GOOGLE –
Business Name Number = 28/1
Founded - September 4, 1988
Day- 4
Power Number – 3 (9+4+1988)

My Readings and insights:

As mentioned above, **Number 1 will be benefited by Number 4** and they can do business together. Here both Larry and Sergey have Number 4 and they founded Google on day 4 and Google name adds to 1. In fact, as partners also their numbers align and are in harmony.

Note that, Number 1 gets benefitted by Number 4 and vice-versa. The colors of the logo of Google are the lucky colors of Number 1.

Google's value as of May 2017 was $101.8 B.

This is a perfect example of what happens when the business name is in harmony with its founder's lucky numbers. So, if you are starting your business, then think of date of incorporation, colors of your logo, name number, and your personal lucky numbers.

AS SUGGESTED EARLIER, USE DAY NUMBER, POWER NUMBER, ZODIAC SIGN, IT'S RULING PLANET, ITS NUMBER, AND THEN DECIDE A NAME AND CAREER.

The other point to keep in mind is the hidden meaning of the numbers that adds to 1.

Here Google adds to 28 and that adds to 1. (Please note how Larry Page's day number is 8 and they both have 4 with them. Numbers 2,4, and 8 are family). You may ask that what is the meaning of Number 28.

Number 28 provides very fast progress by way of final number 1. But the presence of 28 does bring struggles, legal battles and unexpected losses. So, care needs to be taken to ensure that sudden progress and recognition is not lost easily.

To sum up, Number 1 is all about leadership, power, recognition, comforts, and someone who wants to lead the crowd and not be part of the crowd. The lucky colors, dates, and letters for naming the business will provide better chances of success.

Summing up -

- **Step 1** - Find the meaning of your day of birth, strengths and weakness
- **Step 2** - Find out the meaning of your power number by adding all the numbers of your birthdate. Pick the career or job or business as per the final number and your interests.
- **Step 3** - Find out your name number values and its meanings. If it's lucky use it as usual. If it's not, consult a professional to bring it on a more harmonious name number.
- **Step 4** - Find out your personal year and what it might bring.
- **Step 5** - Find out your personal day before you start a job or business or new venture.

- **Step 6** - Find out your lucky days and dates to set up meetings or events to bring success.
- **Step 7** - On a daily basis keep your lucky color and solutions with you. Either in your clothing or wallet/handbag or take a circle shape of yellow cloth or construction paper and write your day number 1,10,19 or 28 on it in yellow color (don't worry even if you can't see it) and put it in your wallet/handbag.
- **Bonus** - Number 1 people will face some health or career issues, so wear golden Topaz 3-5 carats on the right hand right finger in a gold ring. Ruby also will give you great results. If cost is a concern, then follow Step 7.

(Do consult a professional number-influencer before you follow any recommendations for the most beneficial results)

"Born into poverty to a teenage mother on January 29 (<u>adds to number 11/2</u>), went through rough childhood and teenage, found her breakthrough at the age of 19 (adds to number 1) and rose to unimaginable fame, dubbed the "Queen of All Media", ranked the richest African-American, the greatest black philanthropist in American history, North America's first multi-billionaire black person and the HOST of the highest rated television talk show one of its kind in the history "The Oprah Winfrey Show".

- Meet OPRAH WINFREY

Another example of extraordinary success of number 2 is of Tony Robbins, born on February 29, 1960 (day 29 adds to 11/2).

CHAPTER 2 - ALL ABOUT NUMBER 2

Number 2 people are dreamers and very creative. Planet Moon is the ruling planet. Impact of the Moon makes them imaginative and very emotional. Just like the different phases of the moon, they also go through a lot of changes in their life.

Day Number 2 -
Those born on 2nd, 11th and 29th of any given month are Number 2 personalities. The day number is the key to understanding your talents and strengths.

Power Number aka Life Purpose -
Those born on any date of any given month but having the power number 2 are also Number 2 personalities. It is the key to finding which business or career will bring you success.

Zodiac Ruler -
If your zodiac sign is Cancer, then you are ruled by Planet Moon and number 2. Knowing the ruling planet can help you either maximize the beneficial results of your lucky number or minimize the harmful effects of unlucky number influence. This is usually done by the name change.

Name Number -
If the alphabet values in your name add to 2, then you are ruled by Number 2 too.

Characteristics -
The influence of the Moon makes them inquisitive, intuitive and research-oriented. I have seen many explorers and adventurers of the mystic world with this number.

They are ruled by the mind power and are blessed with intelligence, uniqueness and inner wisdom. They find peace if they can balance their passion with their purpose. The satisfaction of bringing value is key to them.

Due to the strong placement of Moon, they might come up with the revolutionary ideas and even start a new religion or spiritual movement. But whatever they do, they bring their intelligence, intuition and passion. Some great examples are of Mahatma Gandhi, Oprah Winfrey, and Gabrielle Bernstein.

You can call them the leaders, preachers, and guru of the unconventional thought.

One of the best examples would be of **Oprah Winfrey**. No other television show in the history of national television stayed number 1 for 25 years. The show was a huge success because of Oprah's originality and unconventional ideas. In fact, her talk show was intention-based. Number 2 attains success when they find a balance of their intellect and intuition.

The Sun showers its light upon the moon and moon shines it upon others. Number 2 people go through phases till they find their inner wisdom and power. Once Number 2 personalities achieve that; they shine their inner wisdom, will power and new ideas upon the world. In fact, self-awareness and self-confidence brings them their shine. However, they do not achieve success without facing failures, trials, struggles and denial from their surroundings.

The trials and tribulations make them skeptic of trusting others and even themselves. They thrive when they find their mentors just like Sun shines the light upon the Moon, and the Moon reflects it back upon the world. The moment they find their mentor, guru, teacher, and inner guide, they take-off. The new Number 2 personality starts to shine its amazing power and light of wisdom.

Remember your personality is the mix of all the numbers of your date of birth and not just the day number.

Due to their artistic nature, they lack practical approach to life and suffer confusion, indecisiveness and become argumentative or submissive. They need balance, and that can be achieved by meditation, yoga, prayers, and having a mentor in life.

So, you will find them very honest and trustworthy or doubtful and untrustworthy. For Number 2 people, the saying that "as the company, so the color" is very accurate. One should caution against bad company and try to be very mindful of friends and friendship.

They are great in talking themselves out of situations, but over-thinking and overanalyzing can cause harm to them. Procrastination needs to be overcome by self-confidence. Due to overthinking, they become lazy and lack the motivation. If you could get them to do anything without arguments, then you are the boss!

Their mind controls their life. If they can set high goals for their life, cultivate self-trust, confidence, strong will power and trust their intuition early on in their life, then that will save them a lot of failures, struggles, and misery.

LIGHTBULB: This is where numerology can help them tremendously. By making sure that their name is in harmony with the lucky numbers, using lucky colors, and doing important things on lucky dates, they can turn the course of their life and achieve impossible feats.

Now knowing the two extremes of number 2, one can start focusing on a positive aspect of sharp intellect, intuition, meditation and channeling that energy for the benefit of the masses. Most of the spiritual gurus', masters, preachers, visionaries, and thought-leaders share this number. That is a perfect example of harnessing the positive power of Number 2.

Another drawback is that they find very hard to have true friends. No matter how hard they try, no matter how much they help others, their friends will hardly appreciate or be grateful for that. However, if they make friends with either 1,3,4,7 and 8, then they will always be there for them to help, support, and empower them.

However, friendship with those under 2,11, 20 or 29 will start very fast but will eventually result in bitterness or enmity. So, avoid that. Number 2 personalities will be very close to and great friends with those with number 7.

They need to learn to trust and appreciate the love of their near and dear ones. If they want to have a happy life, then control over-thinking, finding faults with others, and not argue unnecessarily.

Specific characteristics: Apart from this, there might be few specific characteristics as per their actual day of birth. I am giving some more insight below-

Day Number 2 –
This number makes you imaginative, great counsellor and you live with high ideals. However, you need to learn to maintain your temper and focus in one area. The should use their power in writing or public speaking for a more rewarding and fulfilling career.

Day Number 11 –
This number makes your god-fearing, religious, and faithful to you, your family and in the creator. Even if left without support, your inner instinct will guide you and your confidence will take you to unimaginable heights. I have seen this number thrives in career or industry related to sports!

Day Number 20 –
These are the healers, preachers and leaders who have massive following. The world sees them as divine incarnation. Their ideas are usually ground-

breaking and unconventional but they earn fame and wealth by following their calling.

Day Number 29 –
Those born on 29th are have two faces. One of someone who is very selfish, rude and would only do things for personal gain. The second is of someone who is torn between family number 2 and public calling – number 9 and thus the life will always have some challenges. They are great in arguments and also in public speaking. Thus, many legal professionals are from this area and they are pretty good too. OPRAH WINFREY is a classic public-speaking hall of fame example with number 29.

Various variations of Name Number 2 series
(How to calculate name number is shown in the section titled "Introduction")

As mentioned previously, if the name number adds to 2 series, then you will be under the influence of Number 2 too. Below are the specific characteristics of various variations of Name Number 2.

Name Number 11 - This number will make you a sacrificial goat. They rise by their faith in the Universe and self-confidence. However, the key to success is to follow their instinct and be respectful to all.

Name Number 20 - This is a very fortunate number for those who want to attain great success in the spiritual field. Their personal success comes from serving the masses, helping other lead a better life, solving misery, and the medical professionals, social workers and religious heads have this number.

Name Number 29 - Due to the presence of 2 and 9, they face lot of legal battles and hardships in the life. Here is something I have noticed that they either have good personal life or professional life but not both. I would not recommend having this as a name number.

Name Number 38 - This name number brings success and support from others. They achieve success, fame and name. But the sudden advancement can also lead to sudden downfall and end in personal or professional life.

Name Number 47 - This number brings sudden advancement in career or business and success. However, they seem to suffer mental stress and health issues especially eye-problems.

NOTE: Name number that adds to after 55 can be reduced to the next number series.

Lucky Dates -
For those with the influence of ruling planet Moon by way of Number 2, their lucky dates are 7, 16, and 25 of every month. These dates should be observed for all important meetings, events, launch of business, job interviews, and trading.

Fortunate events take place on these dates. Care should be taken to follow these dates on a consistent basis. The more you follow these dates, the more positive impact you will see in your life. These dates will culminate in events that will bring success.

Dates of 1,10, 19 and 28 will also bring positive results. In fact, these dates might bring great favors to you and support from others.

Your dates of 2,11,20, and 29 will bring mixed results and could be eventful at times. So, avoid using 2, 20 and 29.

<u>If you follow number 11 as the dual power of Number 1-The Sun, then the sky is the limit for you.</u> Do all important things on 11 and consider not as 2 but the dual power of the planet Sun.

Unlucky Dates -
The unlucky dates provide support to unfavorable events and bring misfortune, setbacks, and struggles. You should avoid doing any important task or business on dates adding to 8,9,17, 18, 26, and 27. This rule should be followed power number of 8 and 9 too. That is adding the entire date and if the final result is 8 or 9, then avoid those dates.

Success Mantra -
Anything they do, if they do with honesty, integrity, sincerity, and faith in the higher being, that will bring them abundance and great fortune. In fact, their life will become a rags-to-riches story. So, trusting their inner wisdom, faith in God and surrendering to the Universe is the key to their success.

They can be great preachers, lawyers, painters, artists, musicians, and writers. The occult science could also be their brand icon. Remember perseverance and trust is the key to their success journey.

Business in publication, trading, sports equipment and supplies, clothes, photography, and media can also bring them success.

Persons born on 11th will always excel in sports and games. They have to trust their intuition, intellect, and imagination. Give up their over thinking, procrastination, and get going on their dream path.

Business Relationships -
Number 2 people should partner only with those having either 1,3,4, or 7 numbers. However, please remember that other numbers of your date of birth should be considered too.

Suppose, your date of birth is 2nd June 1982. In this case, day number is 2, and power number is 1. Thus, here Number 1 will be very beneficial. But if the date of birth was 4th June 1981, then the day number is 4, and power number is 11/2. Then do not use 4 even though 4 could be a good business partner. The reason being by using number 4, you are boosting the power of 4 and 4 brings limitations in life. You should use 1 and avoid 2 and 4.

Great Advice - Number 2 and 7 will always be great for each other and numbers 1,3,4, and 8 will support too.

One rule won't apply to everyone, just like one hat doesn't fit all. The numbers have to be analyzed of each person separately and then decide what is most beneficial by keeping in mind the day, life path, name and zodiac number along with handwriting, palmistry and birth time.

Line of work -
Number 2 being an imaginative, creative, gifted, talented as well romantic personality, they could do great things in the media & entertainment industry. In fact, top movie producers, actors, and actresses have this number with them.

Number 2 people make great writers, orators, counselors, lawyers, creative fields, sports, manufacturing as well management of textiles, beverages, fresh produce and their intuition can help them carve careers in mystic world too.

Personal Relationships –

They seem to not have a happy life if they marry those in number series of 2 and 7. Although, they are naturally drawn to these numbers. However, they are both imaginative numbers so a woman marrying a number 1 man can be a good support. A number 2 marrying another number 2 would have an unhappy relationship. Marrying a number 7 could lead them to court or separation. However, I do not recommend a number 2 marrying another number 2. Marriage seems to be a challenge but if married to number 4 and 1 could be much better.

NOTE: No matter how great the numbers are, if the marriage date is not lucky; the results could be adverse. So, keep that in mind before selecting a date. Use your lucky dates for that purpose too.

Lucky Colors -
The colors create an aura just like the aura of each human being. If you are boosting your lucky aura, the positive things will happen. For Number 2 people, light green is extremely fortunate. They should use this color in their clothing every day. In fact, in business cards, d cor, logo, name, and other things around them.

Then comes the light shades of yellow and white. These colors will strengthen the positivity and will help achieve success by bringing favorable events to life.

Unlucky Colors -
Avoid red, black, and dark blue at all times. I can't emphasize enough that by using these colors, you bring more of unfavorable events in your life. Improvise to grow richness and joy in your life.

Precious Stones & Gems-
Pearl and silver can bring success to them. That will also provide beneficial effects upon their health as usually, they suffer from stomach related issues such as indigestion, constipation, asthma, mucus, gas troubles and upper respiratory problems.

Solutions-
    If you are facing health issues, wear Pearl in a ring or a pendant.
    If you are facing financial issues, give something in charity on Monday.
    Have pet cats in the house and feed them milk every day. It will bring favorable results.
    You can also donate every month white sweets to a needy or to an orphanage.
    You can keep a square of silver or a small piece of crystal in your wallet or purse and see if it brings positive results.
    Use silver utensils or at least drink water in silver glass every day.
    Avoid eating meat on Monday or dates of 2,11 and 20.
    Meditation and yoga would be great for you.
    Wear your lucky colors on a daily basis.
    Set up important meetings or interview on your lucky days or dates.

Alphabets representing Number 2
B, K, and R have the value of Number 2. So, care should be taken in naming your business that starts with either of these alphabets.

Remember each alphabet is a numerical impact of its planet. Knowing the impact that it brings, you should be careful in creating that result in your life, your business, and your career.

Here are few references to top famous names to illustrate that how their success is the result of numbers.

Power Names	Date of Birth	Day & Power Numbers
LI KA-SHING- CHAIRMAN, CK HUTCHISON HOLDINGS	JULY 29, 1928	2 & 2
CHARLES KOCH- CEO, KOCH INDUSTRIES	NOVEMBER 1, 1935	1 & 2
LEE SHAU KEE –	JANUARY 29, 1928	2 & 5
OPRAH WINFREY	JANUARY 29, 1954	2 & 4
GABBY BERNSTEIN	NOVEMBER 1, 1979	1 & 2
WAYNE DYER	MAY 10, 1940	1 & 2
TONY ROBBINS	FEBRUARY 29, 1960	2 & 2

Companies with Name Number 2
(source- http://fortune.com/global500/list/)

Company name	Name Number
UNITED HEALTH GROUP	29/2
DAIMLER	20/2
ALPHABET	29/2

People with Name Number 2

Power Names	Name Number
GEORGE SOROS	47/2

Now let's see how you can use this information to create your business/personal success. I am explaining about **Oprah Winfrey** here.

Now see the **NUMBERS** of the important events in OPRAH WINFREY's life:

Example:

Name Number = Oprah Winfrey = 6
Date of birth – 29th January, 1954 =
Day Number =29/2
Power Number = 4(29+1+1954)
Zodiac Sign = Aquarius (ruling planet Uranus/Saturn, ruling number 4 and 8)
Oprah is born on FRIDAY- Ruling Planet Venus- Number 6
So, Oprah Winfrey has ruling numbers of 2,4, 8,6
Now see how her lucky NUMBERS impacted OPRAH WINFREY's life:

1960 - Moved to Milwaukee at age 6 adds to "number 6"
1968 - Ran away from her home in 1968 adds to "number 6"
1970 - Won a scholarship to Tennessee State University in 1970 adds to" number 8 "
1971- Crowned Miss Black Tennessee at age 17 adds to "number 8"
1976 - Moved to Baltimore to host the show at the age 22 adds to "number 4"
1978 - Moved from news anchor to the WJZ-TV morning show at the age 24 adds to "number 6"
1983 - Moved to Chicago, Illinois to host the AM Chicago show at the age 29 adds to "number 2"
1984 - Extremely successful and first episode of AM Chicago released in 1984 adds to "number 4"
1985 - Nominated for Academy Award for THE COLOR PURPLE at the age 31 adds to" number 4"
1987 - Won her first Emmy for her talk show at the age 33 adds to "number 6"
1988 - Named the Broadcaster of the Year in 1988 adds to "number 8"
1992 - Won Best Talk Show Host at the Daytime Emmy Awards at the age 38 adds to "number 2"
1995 - Became the first woman and the only black on Forbes list of 400 richest Americans in 1995 adds to "number 6"
1997 - Formed Oprah Angel Network in 1997 adds to "number 8"
1998 - Formed Oxygen Media, received Lifetime Achievement Award at the age 44 adds to "number 8"
2002 - Launched the O Magazine and became the recipient of the first Bob Hope Humanitarian Award in 2002 adds to "number 4"
2004 - Named by Time as one of the 100 people who most influenced the 20th Century in 2004 adds to "number 6"
2005 - Became the first black listed by Businessweek as one of America's 50 most generous philanthropist at the age 51 adds to "number 6"
2006 - Signed 3-year contract with XM Radio and Forbes listed her as the world's only black billionaire in 2006 adds to "number 8"

2011 - Started her OWN network in 2011 adds to "number 4"
2013 - Awarded the Presidential Medal of Freedom in 2013 adds to "number 6"
This is a perfect example of how ruling numbers were her best years and changed the course of her life. It's all about NUMBERS.

Summing up -

- **Step 1** - Find the meaning of your day of birth, strengths and weakness
- **Step 2** - Find out the meaning of your power number by adding all the numbers of your birthdate. Pick the career or job or business as per the final number and your interests.
- **Step 3** - Find out your name number values and its meanings. If it's lucky use it as usual. If it's not, consult a professional to bring it on a more harmonious name number.
- **Step 4** - Find out your personal year and what it might bring.
- **Step 5** - Find out your personal day before you start a job or business or new venture.
- **Step 6** - Find out your lucky days and dates to set up meetings or events to bring success.
- **Step 7** - On a daily basis keep your lucky color and solutions with you. Either in your clothing or wallet/handbag or take a circle shape of white cloth or construction paper and write your day number 2,11,20 or 29 on it in white color (don't worry even if you can't see it) and put it in your wallet/handbag.
- **Bonus** - Number 2 people will face some health or career or relationship issues, so wear Pearl 3-5 carats in a silver ring. Cat's eye and Jade also will give you great results. If cost is a concern, then follow Step 7.

(Do consult a professional number-influencer before you follow any recommendations for the most beneficial results)

"Born on <u>January 12 (adds to 3)</u>, 1964; early on in his life, this young man had interest in computers and technology. After graduating from Princeton, he worked on the Wall Street and had a great career. But noticed the upcoming change and took that opportunity. After making a cross-country drive from New York to Seattle, he wrote up the business plan and set up the company in his garage on July 5, 1994 at the <u>Age of 30 (adds to number 3)</u>. He left his well-established career and worked his way up to become the richest man in the world. He is an American entrepreneur, computer-scientist, philanthropist, founder, chairman and CEO of AMAZON".

- Meet JEFF BEZOS- One of the richest man in the world

Another example of extraordinary success of Number 3 is Warren Buffett, born on August 30, 1930 (day 30 adds to 3).

CHAPTER 3 - ALL ABOUT NUMBER 3

One word that sums up Number 3 is "Everything is possible". The ruling planet is Jupiter (the planet of wealth). They represent the common man and the concerns of common man. Their strength is their relentless energy to do anything, especially in business.

Day Number 3 -
Those born on 3rd, 12th, 21st and 30th of any given month are Number 3 personalities. The day number is the key to understanding your talents and strengths.

Power Number aka Life Purpose -
Those born on any date of any given month but having the power number 3 are also Number 3 personalities. It is the key to finding which business or career will bring you success.

Zodiac Ruler -
If your zodiac sign is Sagittarius, then you are ruled by Planet Jupiter. Knowing the ruling planet can help you either maximize the beneficial results of your lucky number or minimize the harmful effects of unlucky number influence. This is usually done by the name change.

Name Number -
If the alphabet values in your name add to 3, then you are ruled by Number 3 too.

Characteristics -
They are hardworking, sincere, full of zeal, and honest. Even though they might amass great wealth or lose their wealth, they won't bother but their honor, respect, and self-esteem is their biggest possession. They don't hesitate to introduce their ideas and opinions. However, their outside persona might be different and others might think that they are strict, rude and arrogant but inside they are down to earth and religious.

Their success comes from starting a venture that solves a social problem or serves a social cause. Due to their perseverance, hard work and trusting to inner instinct, they achieve great heights in life and attain fame.

Now there might be few who are number 3 but don't show this characteristic. This is either due to the weak placement of planet Jupiter or due to other numbers in you date of birth or the negative name number.

They are straightforward and always speaking their minds. You cannot change their mind if they already made a decision. This habit of speaking their mind without thinking of others or listening to others might bring them downfall or legal battles in the latter half of the life. It also brings them many enemies.

Remember dignity and honor means a lot to them. Hence they do not like to waste time or their words on something they don't believe in or don't want to do.

Number 3 makes resonate well with inner wisdom, and they get along well with their compatible partners.

Specific characteristics: Apart from this, there might be few specific characteristics as per their actual day of birth. I am giving some more insight below-

Day Number 3 -
Being a single digit number 3, they will shine in life but in the latter half. Their focus is on their creation of something new or the start of a new venture. They often ignore their family in the greed for achieving more. Meditation would do wonders for them.

Day Number 12 –
This number 12 is not a fortunate one although it does succeed albeit after a lot of personal sacrifices! They are blessed with the gift of gab, but they face a lot of struggles early on in life. A business that serves the society will bring the success.

Day Number 21 –
Similarly with this Number 21, they struggle a lot, and they are always thinking of their own good. This attitude breeds enmity and success come after lot of struggle but with their determination, hard work, and perseverance.

Day Number 30 –
This number is carrying a 0. Anytime there is the presence of "0", remember it will bring lack of something, and a karmic debt needs to be paid before life can show up with the happy gifts. This number is very inquisitive, daring, selfish and take things as per their whim and fancy. They will find success in research and investigative fields as well as creative work.

VARIOUS VARIATIONS OF NAME NUMBER 3 SERIES

(How to calculate name number is shown in the section titled "Introduction")

As mentioned previously, if the name number adds to 3 series, then you will be under the influence of Number 3 too. Below are the specific characteristics of various variations of Name Number 3.

Name Number 3 - This number will make you popular, bring you a good education, and intelligence. Education will be the key to your success and great comforts.

Name Number 12 - This name number is blessed with the power of speaking. They earn name and fame by using this talent for the upliftment of the society.

Name Number 21 - This name number is a mystic, selfish and full of personal greed. They face hardships in early life but then find permanent success.

Name Number 30 - This number name is a good blend of dreamers and thinkers. They do what they feel is right and their inner wisdom is the key to bringing success.

Name Number 39 - With the presence of number 9, you will be drawn to humanitarian causes, and number 3 will make you creative. So you will achieve success by serving others.

Name Number 48 - Although it is another number 3, but the presence of 8 and 4 is not lucky for them. This name number brings a lot of struggle, failures and personal loss. They will always face some kind of limitations.

Lucky Dates -
Those who have the number 3 influence either by way of a day or power number or name number, they can start using their lucky dates.

These dates are series of 3.
3rd, 12th, 21st, and 30th, is lucky for them.

Friendly Number -
Series of number 9 such as 9th, 18th, and 27th will be fortunate for you.

Using lucky dates increases chances of success, favorable networking, successful partnerships, and long-lasting positive results.

Try to do your important meetings, events, deals and efforts on your lucky number series.

Unlucky Dates -
Series of number 6 is not fortunate to them. Thus, dates 6th, 15th and 24th of any given month should be avoided.

Line of Work -
Number 3 personalities gain name, fame and wealth by working in banks, schools, universities, senior administrative roles, business, sales, and social service.

Number 3 can also make a living by working in government jobs or as a consultant. However, the presence of other numbers needs to consider too.

Remember using this information can help you decide which areas are suitable for you as per your day number or power number to get name and fame!

Business Partners -
Number 2,3 and 9 series people will always be with them and help.

Personal Relationships -
In a personal relationship, you might be happy if married to people from number 3 or 9 series. Even number 2 series is helpful to you.
However, I do not recommend any other number of 1,4,5,6, and 8 at all, as this usually ends up in arguments, difficulties, separation, childless problems, and struggles.

Lucky Colors -
From using your lucky colors in your d cor, personal clothing, a business logo to anything, the possibilities are endless. This is an easy way to get maximum benefit from your lucky numbers by using the relevant lucky colors in your daily life.

Lucky colors for number 3 are shades of orange, pink and purple.

Unlucky Colors -
Avoid dark blue, green and black at all times.

Precious stones & metal -
Yellow sapphire is usually good for them, but Amethyst can be used too.

Solutions-

If you are facing health issues, use Yellow Sapphire in ring or pendant.

If you are facing financial issues, give something in charity on Thursday and wear Amethyst in a ring.

Have pet birds in the house and feed them every day. It will bring favorable results.

You can also donate every month bananas and sweets to a needy or to an orphanage.

You can keep a circle of yellow cloth in your wallet or handbag and write your day number 3 ,21 or 30 on it or a piece of turmeric and see if it brings positive results.

Using turmeric in everyday meal would be good for you.

Avoid eating meat on Thursday or dates of 3,12,21 and 30.

Meditation and yoga would be great for you.

Wear your lucky colors on a daily basis.

Set up important meetings or interview on your lucky days or dates.

IMPORTANT THINGS TO REMEMBER -

These English alphabets have been given the value of number 3:

Letter C, G, L and S

Companies with Name Number 3
(source- http://fortune.com/global500/list/)

Company name	Name Number

WALMART	21/3
SAMSUNG ELECTRONICS	30/3
AMAZON.COM	39/3
TOYOTA MOTOR	48/3
CHINA CONSTRUCTION BANK	75/3
MICROSOFT	39/3

People with Name Number 3

Meet Jeff Bezos
Born on **January 12, 1964**, as a child he was always curious on how things work. During high school, he started his first business of an educational summer camp and after graduating in computer science, he worked at pretty big names to eventually becoming a youngest vice president. With that successful career, he decided to take a RISK of moving into e-commerce in 1994 and opened an online bookstore by launching his company in his garage and soon named that AMAZON.COM on **July 16, 1995**. (Personal day **6**) That idea made him the richest man with the net worth of $93.7 billion.

What made Jeff Bezos? If your answer is hard work, then think again. 95% of the world population lives from paycheck to paycheck and works very hard but their worth is not $93.7 billion!!

There is something, I noticed there is a similarity in many Forbes topper. Their numbers. In Numerology, there are few numbers that always seem to make it BIG, no matter what. These numbers are **1,3, 5, and 6.**

Add the birth date of Jeff Bezos-
January 12, 1964
1 (January is 1st month)
3 (add 12)- Day Number also called Tools
20 (add 1964)
6(total adds to 1+3+20)- Power Number

Jeff Bezos has two of the lucky numbers **Day 3** (add 12) and **Power Number 6** (total of all the numbers in your date of birth)-6

Jeff Bezos Name Number is –

JEFF   BEZOS
1588   25773 = 46=10=**1**

AMAZON
141775 = 25= **7**

Number 3 people like Number 1 people are very ambitious, they are disciplined, get things done and expect others to obey them too just like they follow to the T!

They usually rise in their life and find a solution to make their situations better. One of the richest person, Warren Buffett born on August 30th Day 3) use to throw newspapers from one house to the other. Another number 3 example is of Tom Cruise born on July 3, 1962! He went through roller-coaster ride but managed to shine again.

That is the magic of Planet Jupiter, number 3!

Summing up -

- **Step 1** - Find the meaning of your day of birth, strengths and weakness

- **Step 2** - Find out the meaning of your power number by adding all the numbers of your birthdate. Pick the career or job or business as per the final number and your interests.
- **Step 3** - Find out your name number values and its meanings. If it's lucky use it as usual. If it's not, consult a professional to bring it on a more harmonious name number.
- **Step 4** - Find out your personal year and what it might bring.
- **Step 5** - Find out your personal day before you start a job or business or new venture.
- **Step 6** - Find out your lucky days and dates to set up meetings or events to bring success.
- **Step 7** - On a daily basis keep your lucky color and solutions with you. Either in your clothing or wallet/handbag or take a circle shape of yellow cloth or construction paper and write your day number 3,21 or 30 on it in orange color (don't worry even if you can't see it) and put it in your wallet/handbag.
- **Bonus** - Number 3 people are lucky and can face some health issues. They can wear Amethyst or Yellow Sapphire of 3-5 carats on the index finger of left hand for consistent luck and success. If cost is a concern, then follow Step 7.

(Do consult a professional number-influencer before you follow any recommendations for the most beneficial results)

"Born on June 4, 1990, (day 4) this young boy had a passion for design, technology and computers. It was during product design class at Stanford, he proposed Snapchat as a project. The idea creation was done sometime in April, 2011 (month 4, year adds to 4) The idea then ridiculed but trusting his instinct, he left Stanford in 2012 to focus on his project. That one decision made him the youngest BILLIONAIRE in the world in 2015".

- Meet Evan Thomas Spiegel, an American Internet entrepreneur, co-founder and CEO of SnapChat

Another example of extraordinary success of number 4 is of Harry Potter fame writer, J.K. Rowling, born on July 31, 1965 (day 31 adds to 4)

CHAPTER 4 - ALL ABOUT NUMBER 4

One word that sums up Number 4 is "social reformer of rules." The ruling planet is Uranus. They represent the common man and their concerns. Their strength is their skill to depict details and follow the rules. They are the ones who can move mountains by their sheer grit, hard work, and willpower.

Day Number 4
Those born on 4th,13rd, and 22nd of any given month are Number 4 personalities. The day number is the key to understanding your talents and strengths.

Power Number aka Life Purpose -
Those born on any date of any given month but having the power number 4 are also Number 4 personalities. It is the key to finding which business or career will bring you success.

Zodiac Ruler -
If your zodiac sign is Virgo, then you are ruled by Planet Mercury and planet Uranus (Number 4 and 5). Knowing the ruling planet can help you either maximize the beneficial results of your lucky number or minimize the harmful results of the unlucky number. This can done by the making changes in the way you spell your name and signature patterns.

Name Number -
If the alphabet values in your name add to 4, then you are ruled by Number 4 too.

The BEST NAME NUMBER for you is of number 1 series. This boosts the confidence to achieve anything they want.

Characteristics -
They are great reformers and often do so by introducing their ideas and opinions. This habit of speaking their mind without thinking of others makes them many enemies.

They do not show interest in others and is misunderstood as egotism. Thus, not letting them have many friends. Philosophy, religion, new age science and mysticism appeal to them.

They usually do not desire much from life and are self-content. They like good food, are compassionate, and struggle very hard to earn a living.

In the latter half of their life, they will develop the keen interest in spirituality and social change. However, they do not start a new venture, till they are sure to succeed.

Specific characteristics:

Day Number 4 -
Number 4 born are very conservative, traditional, get irritated easily, brave and must learn to take things in a positive stride.

Day Number 13 –
This number 13 is often taken as a mark of misfortune. They face hardships in early childhood, may face situations due to personal affairs and should learn to be honest.

Day Number 22 –
This Number 22 is the diamond mine of strong will power. Their mind is always **thinking** and sometimes turn to evil. They can thrive in the business that serves the public. They must build connections by being ready for opportunities.

Day Number 31 –
This number is better than all other numbers in 4 series. The 3 makes them creative, and 1 gives them leadership with ambitions. This makes them extraordinary, and they do what they decide to do! They are spiritual and often get into affairs outside of the relationship. The key to their success is to help others succeed.

VARIOUS VARIATIONS OF NAME NUMBER 4 SERIES
(How to calculate name number is shown in the section titled "Introduction")

As mentioned previously, if the name number adds to 4 series, then you will be under the influence of Number 4 too. Below are the specific characteristics of various variations of Name Number 4.

Name Number 4 - This number will make you popular but won't bring luck. They are a powerhouse of knowledge, but their own fears hold them back from their success!!!

Name Number 13 - This number may bring bitter experiences in life and difficulties because of opposite sex. Although they manage to have some success but life will always bring some kind of struggles too.

Name Number 22 - This number makes one fickle-minded, prone to women, drinking, gambling, and evil thoughts. This might bring bad name, and although they are good administrators, they are never satisfied with life.

Name Number 31 - This personality only cares for freedom as per their wish. They show interest in mystic world and philosophy. They earn name and fame but lose all too. Getting it all back takes years. However, if they have a lucky birth number, the life will be a success.

Name Number 40 - Friends are key to your success and positions in life. Stability comes to you as well wealth. But eventually, they lose all. Their life is a constant struggle.

Name Number 49 - This number brings fortune and fame. This number leads to travel, great experiences and sudden change in fortune. This number also brings sudden downfall.

Lucky dates -
Those who have the number 4 influence either by way of a day or power number or name number, they can start using their lucky dates.

These dates are series of 1.
1st, 10th, and 19th is lucky for them.
Notice how I avoid 28th here as experience shows it does not bring great results.

The dates of 4 series may bring sudden changes.

Friendly number -
Series of number 9 such as 9th, 18th, and 27th will be helpful to you.

Using lucky dates increases chances of success, favorable networking, successful partnerships, and long-lasting positive results.

Try to do your important meetings, events, deals and efforts on your lucky number series.

Unlucky Dates -
Series of number 8 is not favorable to them. Thus, dates 8th, 17th and 26th of any given month should be avoided. They should avoid the dates of the number 4 series.

Also, dates such as 7th and 16th and 25th should be avoided too.

Line of Work -
Number 4 personalities gain name, fame and wealth by public speaking, voicing revolutionary thoughts, technological ideas, and opinions. Research of spiritual ideas, public relations, writing, training in the fitness business, organized technology, music, and medicine will be good too.

Number 4 makes a living by serving the public, advising, and helping for a social cause. They should pick the line of work where they can use their mental strength, knowledge and willpower. They have to work very hard and struggle to earn a living.

Remember using this information can help you decide which areas are suitable for you as per your day number or power number to get name and fame!

Business Partners -
Number 1 and 8 series people will always be with them and help.

People with 2 and 4 are also helpful to them.

Personal Relationships -
In a personal relationship, you might be happy if married to people from number 1 or 8 series.

However, I do not recommend any other number of 2, 3,5,6, 7 or 9 as this usually ends up in arguments, difficulties, separation, childless problems, and struggles.

Lucky Colors -
From using your lucky colors in your d cor, personal clothing, a business logo to anything, the possibilities are endless. This is an easy way to get maximum benefit from your lucky numbers by using the relevant lucky colors in your daily life.

Lucky colors for number 4 are all lighter shades of blue and yellow.

Unlucky Colors -
Avoid black at all times.

Precious stones & metal -
Hessonite will bring them good luck, career stability, health, and support.

Solutions-
If you are facing health issues, use Hessonite in ring or pendant.
If you are facing financial issues, start feeding birds daily.
Having pet dogs in the house and feeding them everyday will bring favorable results.
You can also donate every month something to a needy or to an orphanage.
You can keep a peacock feather in your wallet or purse or a circle of silver in your pocket every day for favorable results.
Drink in a silver glass every day.
Avoid eating meat completely.
Wear your lucky colors on a daily basis.
Set up important meetings or interview on your lucky days or dates.

IMPORTANT THINGS TO REMEMBER -

These English alphabets have been given the value of number 4:

Letter D, M, and T

Companies with Name Number 4
(source- http://fortune.com/global500/list/)

Company name	Name Number
SINOPEC GROUP	31/4
INDUSTRIAL & COMMERCIAL BANK OF CHINA	31/4

People with Name Number 4

Power Names	Name Number
WARREN BUFFETT	31/4
CARLOS SLIM HELU	49/4
LARRY ELLISON	31/4

Summing up -

- **Step 1** - Find the meaning of your day of birth, strengths, and weakness.
- **Step 2** - Find out the meaning of your power number by adding all the numbers of your birthdate. Pick the career or job or business as per the final number and your interests.
- **Step 3** - Find out your name number values and its meanings. If it's lucky use it as usual. If it's not, consult a professional to bring it on a more harmonious name number.
- **Step 4** - Find out your personal year and what it might bring.
- **Step 5** - Find out your personal day before you start a job or business or new venture.
- **Step 6** - Find out your lucky days and dates to set up meetings or events to bring success.
- **Step 7** - On a daily basis keep your lucky color and solutions with you. Either in your clothing or wallet/handbag or take a square shape of dark blue cloth or construction paper and write your day 4, 22, 31 on it in light blue color and put it in your wallet/handbag.
- **Bonus** - Number 4 people create their luck and can face some health issues. They can wear Hessonite of 5 carats in the ring overall luck and success. If cost is a concern, then follow Step 7.

(Do consult a professional number-influencer before you follow any recommendations for the most beneficial results)

"Born on May 14, 1984, (adds to Day 5, Month 5, Year 22/4 makes his total 14/5. He is number 5 Trio !!) On February 4th, 2004, this 19-year-old did something that changed the blueprint of social communication. He created "Facebook" and dropped out of Harvard to take his platform to the big heights. Indeed, he did and it made his current worth over $55 Billion".

- Meet MARK ZUCKERBERG, American computer programmer, Internet entrepreneur, co-founder, current chairman and CEO of Facebook.

Another example of extraordinary success of number 5 is of President Donald Trump, born on June 14, 1946 (Day 14 adds to 5)

CHAPTER 5 - ALL ABOUT NUMBER 5

This number is a "free bird." Number 5 is a charismatic communicator. Its ruling planet is Mercury. This number is a must for business and trade. Number 5 helps you become popular and well-known in business and public life such as politics.

"MOST OF THE WORLD'S BILLIONAIRES HAVE THE ZODIAC SIGN OF VIRGO-NUMBER 5"

Day Number 5 -
Those born on 5th, 14th, and 23rd of any given month are Number 5 personalities. The day number is the key to understanding your talents and strengths.

Power Number aka Life Purpose -
Those born on any date of any given month but having the power number 5 are also Number 5 personalities. It is the key to finding which business or career will bring you success.

Zodiac Ruler -
If your zodiac sign is Gemini or Virgo, then you are ruled by Planet Mercury and Number 5. Knowing the ruling planet can help you either maximize the beneficial results of your lucky number or minimize the harmful results of an unlucky number. This is usually done making changes in the way your name is spelt.

Name Number -
If the alphabet values in your name adds to 5, then you are ruled by Number 5 too.

Characteristics -
Number 5 helps you lead a magnificent life from the beginning and makes you highly intuitive. The day number 5 will show its impact, but ultimately it's the power number or life destiny number that you will end up with.

Their mind is the speed-mine. The speed of wind is what is the speed of their thoughts and actions. The ideas they come up with are ahead of their generations. They are great at making friends and are very sociable. They cannot tolerate slow work and expect others to be like them. Delay is denied as per their desire.

Building connections come easy to them, and so they become popular with their group.

However, they end up having many love affairs and this usually is short-lived. They enjoy being a free bird, and so any rules make them uncomfortable. They like to dominate the other partner, and they are very blunt. They speak their mind freely and often regret later but sorry is not their kind of word.

That was the positive effect of 5. But if the number 5 has a negative effect, then it makes the person greedy, prone to cheating, recourse to wrong means to make quick money and fickle-minded. That is, they find hard to focus on one project or goal for too long, and this leads to not having any goal.

They do not like to work hard to earn the freedom lifestyle. The key to their success lies in using their talents to benefit the social cause. Destiny seems to reward them 100% for doing so and beyond wildest dreams.

Those who marry 5 should know that change is their game and freedom is their life. They are charmers, strong mental strength, the gift of speaking and intuition to see & know.

Specific characteristics:

Day Number 5 -
Number 5 born have high ideals, live for honor, intuitive and attractive disposition.

Day Number 14 –
This number 14 makes them travelers. They cannot live without traveling. It's oxygen to them. They manage to get success, name, fame, wealth and riches in business. They will always have support, especially from Number 9 series. They should guard against unhealthy eating habits and health.

Day Number 23 –
This Number 23 can make or break anything they put their mind to! They have luck, personality, support, and resources always with them. If the day number or power number or name number is lucky, then the sky's the limit.

VARIOUS VARIATIONS OF NAME NUMBER 5 SERIES
(How to calculate name number is shown in the section titled "Introduction")

As mentioned previously, if the name number adds to 5 series, then you will be under the influence of Number 5 too. Below are the specific characteristics of various variations of Name Number 5.

Name Number 5 - This name number gives charisma, confidence, fame and overspending habit. Try to control the negative aspect.

Name Number 14 - This name number is all about business. This personality is always surrounded by people and busy with traveling. They can become a prominent public figure. The only disadvantage is that family life and love life will always be a challenge. So, take no hasty decisions.

Name Number 23 - This name number sure is destiny's favorite. Anything they do, they succeed. Just remember success is a gift by Universe to you so do not get lazy and be humble.

Name Number 32 - This name number is an intuitive child. This number brings success to their uniqueness, following their ideals, inner wisdom, and by serving the society.

Name Number 41- This name number achieves success, fame and wealth but should not make haste decisions. The loss from hasty decisions could lead to suffering.

Name Number 50 - This name number has zero in it. Thus, life will deliver you one karmic lesson and success will come to you in the later part of your life. Your mind power will bring success to you.

Lucky Dates -
Those who have the number 5 influence either by way of a day or power number or name number, they can start using their lucky dates.

These dates are series of 5 and 9.
5th, 14th, 23rd, 9th, 18th and 27th is lucky for them.

MILLION DOLLAR ADVICE –

Number 5 is a double-edged sword. Although they are blessed with fortunes, personal life will always be a challenge to them. To avoid further misery, do not get married on the dates that add to 5 such as 5th, 14th, and 23rd. This will lead to childlessness or delay in childbirth or miscarriage or separation.

Using lucky dates increases chances of success, favorable networking, successful partnerships, and long-lasting positive results.

Try to do your important meetings, events, deals and efforts on your lucky number series.

Unlucky Dates -
Series of number 3 is not favorable to them. Thus, dates 3rd, 12th, 21st and 30th of any given month should be avoided.

Also, dates such as 7th, 16th and 25th should be avoided.

Line of Work -
Number 5 personalities find success in business and trade. Public support comes easily to them. Even doing agency or franchise work in travel, communications, media, publishing, foreign services, government, and administration will be good for them.

Remember using this information can help you decide which areas are suitable for you as per your day number or power number to get name and fame!

Business Partners -
This is one number that can partner with almost any number series and still be happy.

Personal Relationships -
In a personal relationship, you might be happy if married to people from number 5 but having a child will be difficult.

However, you can marry with the number series of 1,6 and 9.

However, I do not recommend number 2, 3, 7 or 8 as this usually ends up in arguments, difficulties, separation, childless problems, and struggles.

Lucky Colors -
From using your lucky colors in your d cor, personal clothing, a business logo to anything, the possibilities are endless. This is an easy way to get maximum benefit from your lucky numbers by using the relevant lucky colors in your daily life.

Lucky colors for number 5 are all lighter shades especially grey.

Unlucky Colors -
Avoid dark colors especially black and green as these are not favorable for them.

A word of advice- If green is advised to you as a cure based on your spouse's numbers, then use his lucky dates too.

Precious stones & metal -
Diamond will bring them good luck.

Solutions-
If you are facing health issues, use your lucky stone.
If you are facing financial issues, give something in charity on Wednesday.
Have pet birds especially parrot in the house and feed them everyday. It will bring favorable results.
You can also donate every month sweetened milk with rice to a needy or to an orphanage.
You can keep a copper coin in your wallet or purse and see if it brings positive results.
Avoid eating meat and drinking alcohol.
Meditation and yoga would be great for you.
Wear your lucky colors on a daily basis.
Set up important meetings or interview on your lucky days or dates.

IMPORTANT THINGS TO REMEMBER -

These English alphabets have been given the value of number 5:

Letter E, N, H, and X

Companies with Name Number 5
(source- http://fortune.com/global500/list/)

Company name	Name Number
CHINA NATIONAL PETROLEUM	32/5
MCKESSON	32/5
VOLKSWAGEN	41/5
BOEING	23/5

People with Name Number 5

POWER NAMES	NAME NUMBER
JACQUELINE MARS	41/5
WANG JIANLIN	32/5
S. ROBSON WALTON	50/5
JIM WALTON	32/5

Let's look at this example.

Mark Zuckerberg Timeline

Born on May 14, 1984 (Day **5**, Month **5**, Year 22/4 makes his total 14/**5**.
He is **number 5 Trio !!1)**

Personal year (add- day of birth + month of birth + current year = Day 5+Month 5+ 2002/4= 14/5)
2002 (year 4) Age 17(number **8**); Personal year **5** - Joins Harvard University
2003 (Year 5) Age 18 (number 9); Personal year 6 - Launches Facemash
2004(year 6) Age 19 (number 1); Personal year 7 - Starts Thefacebook.com in February Month 2)
2005(Year 7) Age 20 (number 2); Personal year **8** - FB Hits 5 Million users
2006 (Year 8) Age 21 (number 3) Personal year 9 - FB hits 200,000 users; Winklevoss twins file lawsuit
2007(Year 9) Age 22 (number 4); Personal year 1 - Opens FB so anyone with an email can join
2008(Year 10/1) Age 23 (number 5); Personal year 2 - Reaches settlement for $65 million with Winklevoss twins
2009(Year 11/2) Age 24 (number 6); Personal year 3 - China blocks FB access
2010(Year 3) Age 25 (number 7); personal year 4 - Named Time magazine's person of the year; release of movie "The Social Network"

2011 (Year 4) Age 26 (number **8**); Personal year **5** - FB gets half a billion users

2012 (Year 5) Age 27 (number 9; personal year 6 - FB projects 1 billion user mark; Marries Priscilla

2013 (Year 6) Age 28 (number 1); personal year 7 - Zuckerberg became the CEO and Chairman of Facebook

2014(Year 7) Age 29 (number 2); personal year **8** - Dropped out the lawsuits for secluded land on the Hawaiian island of Kauai.

2015(8) Age 30 (number 3); personal year 9 - Couple had daughter Max; announced to give 99% of FB shares to charitable causes

2016(year 9) Age 31 (number **4**); Personal year 1 - He pledged $3 billion to cure the world's diseases by the end of this century

2017(Year 1) Age 32 (number **5**); Personal year 2 - Couple had their second daughter!

Notice how the number 5, 4, and 8 brings him good luck. Number 1, 3, and 6 are friendly too. Number 7 and 9 could bring discomfort.

"On February 4th, 2004, this 19-year-old did something that changed the blueprint of social communication. He created "Facebook" and dropped out of Harvard to take his platform to the big heights. Indeed, he did! Was it just hard work or luck?

I leave with you to contemplate but I found that his numbers are so powerful just like the horsepower of the engine of Ferrari. To me, it's the game of his numbers."

Summing up -

- **Step 1** - Find the meaning of your day of birth, strengths and weakness
- **Step 2** - Find out the meaning of your power number by adding all the numbers of your birthdate. Pick the career or job or business as per the final number and your interests.

- **Step 3** - Find out your name number values and its meanings. If it's lucky use it as usual. If it's not, consult a professional to bring it on a more harmonious name number.
- **Step 4** - Find out your personal year and what it might bring.
- **Step 5** - Find out your personal day before you start a job or business or new venture.
- **Step 6** - Find out your lucky days and dates to set up meetings or events to bring success.
- **Step 7** - On a daily basis keep your lucky color with you. Either in your clothing or wallet/handbag or take a circle shape of grey cloth or construction paper and write your day number 5,14 or 23 on it in grey color don't worry even if you can't see it) and put it in your wallet/handbag.
- **Bonus** - Number 5 people are lucky and can face some health issues. They can wear Diamond or Zircon of 3-5 carats for success. If cost is a concern, then follow Step 7.

(Do consult a professional number-influencer before you follow any recommendations for the most beneficial results)

"BORN ON FEBRUARY 24, 1955 (DAY ADDS TO NUMBER 6), HE WAS BORN TO PARENTS WHO HAD TO PUT HIM FOR ADOPTION AT BIRTH. HE HAD QUITE A ROLLER COASTER RIDE, FROM SLEEPING ON THE FLOOR IN FRIENDS' DORM ROOMS, RETURNING COKE BOTTLES FOR FOOD MONEY, WALKING EVERY WEEK TO GET FREE MEALS AT THE LOCAL HARE KRISHNA TEMPLE TO BECOMING THE BUSINESS TYCOON, INVENTOR, INDUSTRIAL DESIGNER, CHAIRMAN, CO-FOUNDER, CEO, CO-FOUNDER OF APPLE INC, CEO & MAJORITY SHAREHOLDER OF PIXAR AS WELL OF NEXT".

- MEET STEVE JOBS, THE CO-FOUNDER OF OVER $800 BILLION COMPANY, APPLE INC

ANOTHER EXAMPLE OF EXTRAORDINARY SUCCESS OF NUMBER 6 IS OF JAN KOUM, CO-FOUNDER OF WHATSAPP, BORN ON FEBRUARY 24, 1976 (DAY 24 ADDS TO 6)

CHAPTER 6 - ALL ABOUT NUMBER 6

Here comes "the CHARMER". This number 6 rules the media and entertainment world. They are ruled by Planet Venus and have innate ability to charm others.

Day Number 6
Those born on 6th, 15th, and 24th of any given month are Number 6 personalities. The day number is the key to understanding your talents and strengths.

Life Purpose -
Those born on any date of any given month but having the power number 6 are also Number 6 personalities. It is the key to finding which business or career will bring you success.

Zodiac Ruler -
If your zodiac sign is Taurus or Libra, then you are ruled by Planet Venus and Number 6. Knowing the ruling planet can help you either maximize the beneficial results of your lucky number or minimize the harmful results of unlucky number influence. This is usually done by making the changes in the name.

Name Number -
If the alphabet values in your name adds to 6, then you are ruled by Number 6 too.

Characteristics -
Number 6 enjoys great things and luxury in life. The failures, struggles, and delays force them to turn the obstacles around. Their earnest desire to make a name for themselves gets them to work hard and gain a position of power and wealth.

They are entertainers, artists, painters, musicians, and creators who enjoy and appreciate the beauty. Even number 6 homes speak of enchanted beauty.

They also have the gift of gab, and they could easily flatter and falter you!

However, they must learn to be polite and stop humiliating others. They never face lack of basic amenities in their life and always seem to have the money or find ways to fulfill their financial needs.

You would see different shades of Number 6 personalities. Some will be full of positivity, energy and always ready to help. Others will live by high ideals and socialize. This aspect could lead them into extra-marital affairs. But there will those who seem to be enjoying wealth by defrauding, cheating and lying. This group is greedy and disloyal. So, beware!

Specific characteristics:

Day Number 6 - Number 6 born live with high ideals and values. They thrive in creative fields and earn fame.

Day Number 15 - This number 15 makes them great at oratory and winning the gig. Charming and captivating is the key to this number. They manage to be happy-go-lucky.

Day Number 24 - This Number 24 is all-in-all of Number 6. They seem to be destiny's favorite. They have a great family and professional life, earn name and fame as well wealth.

VARIOUS VARIATIONS OF NAME NUMBER 6 SERIES
(How to calculate name number is shown in the section titled "Introduction")

As mentioned previously, if the name number adds to 6 series, then you will be under the influence of Number 6 too. Below are the specific characteristics of various variations of Name Number 6.

Name Number 6 –
This name number brings focus and satisfaction but nothing extraordinary.

Name Number 15 –
This name number is all about making money by hook or crook. With a charming personality and mental strength, they seem to manage all in professional life.

Name Number 24 –
This name number sure is a fortunate one. This helps to gain favors, grow high in positions and earn much wealth.

Name Number 33 –

This name number is the blessings of heaven. Everything seems to be flowing positively in their life. They are spiritually inclined and blessed with abundance.

Name Number 42 –
This number goes through hardships early in life, but then they rise high and settle with riches. The mind power helps them overcome greed and settle with gratitude.

Name Number 51 - This is the most fortunate of this series of 6. This is a highly materialistic number. This is the key to the rags-to-riches success of an ordinary to extraordinary. It is almost like a miracle how this number makes one highly successful. They do not like to be tied to rules and live by their own rule book. This number is the LION-KING of numerology.

Lucky Dates -
Those who have the number 6 influence either by way of a day or power number or name number, they can start using their lucky dates.

These dates are series of 6 and 9.
6th, 15th, 24th, 9th, 18th and 27th is lucky for them.

Using lucky dates increases chances of success, favorable networking, successful partnerships, and long-lasting positive results.

Try to do your important meetings, events, deals and efforts on your lucky number series.

Unlucky Dates -
Series of number 3 is not favorable to them. Thus, dates 3rd, 12th, 21st and 30th of any given month should be avoided. Also, dates such as 5th, 14th and 23rd should be avoided.

Line of Work -
Number 6 personalities are creators and entertainers. They will thrive in fine arts, culinary arts, media, acting, modeling, production, writing, fine jewelry, luxury goods trading, and designers.

Remember using this information can help you decide which areas are suitable for you as per your day number or power number to get name and fame!

Business Partners -
Number 3 people will provide help and are good business partners. So are 6 and 9 number series.

Personal Relationships -
In a personal relationship, you might be happy if married to people from number 1,4,5 and 9 series.

However, I do not recommend number 2, 3, 7 or 8 as this usually ends up in separation, childless problems, and struggles.

Lucky Colors -
From using your lucky colors in your d cor, personal clothing, a business logo to anything, the possibilities are endless. This is an easy way to get maximum benefit from your lucky numbers by using the relevant lucky colors in your daily life.

Lucky colors for number 6 are shades of blue, green and red.

Unlucky Colors -
Lighter colors such as white, yellow and pink are not favorable for them.

Precious Stones & Metal -
Emerald will bring them good luck. Jade and turquoise are also good if you are suffering from stomach issues.

Solutions-
If you are facing health or relationship issues, use your lucky stone.
If you are facing relationship or financial issues, give something in charity on Friday. If you cannot do this, take out a dollar every Friday for donating and then you can use it buy someone free meal or give it away in charity.
You can also donate every month white food or white rice to a needy or to an orphanage.
You can keep a rectangle shape of blue cloth or construction paper and write your day of birth of 6, 15 or 24 on it in green color. Do not worry if you cannot see it. Keep this in your wallet or purse and change it every full moon. If it helps, continue doing it.
Avoid eating meat on Friday or dates of 6, 15, and 24.
For overall benefits, meditate while holding white flowers in your hand and then letting flowers flow in the running water of your kitchen sink. Do this every Friday.
Wear your lucky colors on a daily basis.
Take blessings of your mother.

You usually face relationship issues. To avoid that, always be loyal in your relationships.

IMPORTANT THINGS TO REMEMBER -

These English alphabets have the numeric value of number 6:

Letter U, V, and W

To get the benefit of these letters, the name could begin with either U, V or W.

Companies with Name Number 6
(source- http://fortune.com/global500/list/)

Company name	Name Number
AVIVA	15/6
GLENCORE	33/6
Chevron	**33/6**
BERKSHIRE HATHAWAY	51/6
GENERAL MOTORS	51/6

People with Name Number 6

Power Names	Name Number
PHIL KNIGHT	33/6
DAVID THOMSON	51/6
BEATE HEISTER & KARL ALBRECHT JR.	78/6
DAVID KOCH	33/6
SHELDON ADELSON	60/6
LI KA-SHING	24/6
SERGEY BRIN	24/6

Summing Up -

- **Step 1** - Find the meaning of your day of birth, strengths and weakness
- **Step 2** - Find out the meaning of your power number by adding all the numbers of your birthdate. Pick the career or job or business as per the final number and your interests.
- **Step 3** - Find out your name number values and its meaning. If it's lucky use it as usual. If it's not, consult a professional to bring it on a more harmonious name number.
- **Step 4** - Find out your personal year and what it might bring.
- **Step 5** - Find out your personal day before you start a job or business or new venture.
- **Step 6** - Find out your lucky days and dates to set up meetings or events to bring success.
- **Step 7** - On a daily basis keep your lucky color with you. Either in your clothing or wallet/handbag, take a rectangle shape of blue cloth or construction paper and write your day of birth of 6, 15 or 24 on it in green color don't worry even if you can't see it). Keep this in your wallet or purse and change it every full moon. If it helps continue doing it.
- **Bonus** - Number 6 people are lucky and can face some health issues. They can wear Emerald of 3-5 carats for success. Jade and Turquoise also produce good results. If cost is a concern, then follow Step 7.

(Do consult a professional number-influencer before you follow any recommendations for the most beneficial results)

"Born on December 7, 1956 to a veteran of Korean war, his early life was filled with poverty and hardships. But early on he found his escape in basketball. That passion led him to playing the major leagues and becoming an American professional basketball star legend."

- Meet Larry Bird, American Basketball executive, former coach, and star player

Another example of extraordinary success of number 7 is Xavi Hernandez, the former Barcelona soccer player, born on January 25, 1980 (day 25 adds to 7)

CHAPTER 7 - ALL ABOUT NUMBER 7

Seven is a researcher, inventor and the "FATHER" of the Mystic world. Number 7 personalities are ruled by planet Neptune. They have the power of the divine, the spirit, the instinct and the intuition to turn any obstacle around.

Number 7 is the preacher who thrives on teachings of religion.

Day Number 7 -
Those born on 7th, 16th, and 25th of any given month are Number 7 personalities. The day number is the key to understanding your talents and strengths.

Life Purpose -
Those born on any date of any given month but having the power number 7 are also Number 7 personalities. It's key to find which business or career will bring you success.

Zodiac Ruler -
If your zodiac sign is Cancer, you are ruled by Planet Neptune and Number 7. Knowing the ruling planet can help you either maximize the beneficial results of your lucky number or minimize the harmful results of unlucky number influence. This usually is done by the name change.

Name Number -
If the alphabet values in your name add to 7, then you are ruled by Number 7 too.

Characteristics -
Number 7 is not an extrovert but great orators. They feel comfortable in known surroundings. They usually don't share their feelings easily. They are very creative, and music, arts, oratory, and research is their thing. They are very loyal.

If the power number is 7 or name number is 7, then these people might rise either in politics or preaching. They are very strong, and usually, family life is a challenge. But they make impossible possible ALWAYS!

The mental strength is their power. They seem to worry a lot. They do not follow the conventional path and people seem to follow them easily because of their open communication.

Their life becomes the epitome of success if they use this knowledge to influence and make others life better. They earn it by hard work, sheer grit, and perseverance.

Many gifted people are the gift of this number. They are leaders even if they go through lack of stability in emotional or financial or family or personal life.

However, they succeed when they align their purpose with their strengths. The good karma and deeds show up to find their name and fame.

Specific characteristics:

Day Number 7 -
Number 7 born are artists, creative, religious and God-fearing. They seem to always have some problems. And still, achieve their dreams. They can make things happen but need to live by high ideals.

Day Number 16 –
This number 16 has the mindset of a leader and mental strength is far superior to any other number on the spiritual plane. In fact, most prominent artists, musicians, painters, child wonders and world-class preachers have the backing of this number. With this fame, they might get involved in affairs that could bring them loss and disrespect. This number is a Karmic number. So there will always be challenges and responsibilities.

Day Number 25 –
This Number 25 is a staunch preacher and often start a new cult or religion that becomes very popular. Few of them go on to becoming high-esteemed speakers, teachers, spiritual messengers, church head and great diplomats.

VARIOUS VARIATIONS OF NAME NUMBER 7 SERIES
(How to calculate name number is shown in the section titled "Introduction")

As mentioned previously, if the name number adds to 7 series, then you will be under the influence of Number 7 too. Below are the specific characteristics of various variations of Name Number 7.

Name Number 7 - This name number does not bring materialistic results. In fact, worldly success is often a far chase.

Name Number 16 - If your name number is 16, then please change it asap. This number brings sudden success and speedy downfall.

Name Number 25 - This number demands consistent hard work but brings positive results in the end. They plan their actions before leaping. This foresightedness brings honor and fame.

Name Number 34 - This name number is good for worldly success. However, they usually face problems in the family, or personal life mostly gets defamatory. I strongly suggest changing your name to a luckier number.

Name Number 43 - This name number is torchbearer. The revolutionary who holds to his beliefs, thoughts, and ideas. Although they might get the results in the end, they go through personal loss and end up making many enemies.

Name Number 52 - This name number has the blessings of 5. Hence if supported by other lucky number in the date of birth, this name could create wonders. They earn name and fame for sure. On the personal front, this is not too lucky.

Lucky dates -
Those who have the number 7 influence either by way of a day or power number or name number, they can start using their lucky dates.

These dates are series of 2. 2nd, 11th, 20th, and 29th. Even 25th is lucky for them.
Notice that I am not recommending either 7th or 16th even though it's in their number series because experience shows it doesn't benefit them.

Using lucky dates increases chances of success, favorable networking, successful partnerships, and long-lasting positive results.

Try to do your important meetings, events, deals, and efforts on your lucky number 2 series.

Friendly dates -
The dates of 1st, 10th and 19th will be favorable too in your life. However, notice that I do not recommend 28th as experience shows that it doesn't produce beneficial results. Even number 3 will be supportive.

Unlucky dates -
Dates 7th and 16th of any given month should be avoided as these will add to the misery, struggle, difficulties, and failures.

Also, dates such as 8th, 17th, 26th, and 28th should be avoided.

Line of Work -
Number 7 are innovators and inquisitive kind. They do great in the areas of occult sciences, spiritual teaching, religion, research of any kind and literary work related to these fields. Even in the creative field of media and TV could be great for them. Trading in the luxury items is good too. The business of chemical and medicines is good too.

Remember using this information can help you decide which areas are suitable for you as per your day number or power number to get name and fame!

Business Partners -
Number 7 people have strong mental power. They could do business partnerships with people born under the influence of 1,2,4 and 7.

Personal Relationships -
Their personal life is always a challenge, and they don't benefit from it. In a personal relationship, you might be happy if married to people from number 2 and 4 series only.

However, I do not recommend number 7 or 8 as this usually ends up in separation, childless problems, and failure.

Lucky Colors -
From using your lucky colors in your d cor, personal clothing, a business logo to anything, the possibilities are endless. This is an easy way to get maximum benefit from your lucky numbers by using the relevant lucky colors in your daily life.

Lucky colors for number 7 are white, light yellow, blue and sea green.

Unlucky Colors -
Avoid dark shades of all colors especially black and red.

Precious Stones & Metal -
Cat's eye will bring them good luck. Pearls and Moonstone will be beneficial too.

Solutions-
If you are facing health or relationship issues, use your lucky stone.
If you are facing financial issues, give something in charity on Monday. If you cannot do this, take out a dollar every Monday for donating and then you can use it buy someone free meal or give it away in charity.
You can also donate every month corn kernels or white rice to a needy or to an orphanage.
You can keep a square made of sea green cloth or yellow construction paper and write number 25 on it in sea green color. Do not worry if you cannot see it. Keep this in your wallet or purse and change it every full moon. If it helps continue doing it.
Avoid eating meat on Monday or dates of 7, 16, and 25.
For overall benefits, meditate while holding white flowers in your hand and then letting flowers flow in running water of your kitchen sink. Do this every Monday.
Wear your lucky colors on a daily basis.
You usually face relationship issues. To have a better relationship or find the better one, keep white light lamp on every day in the evening. Keep one on each side of your bed.

IMPORTANT THING TO REMEMBER-

These English alphabets have the value of number 7:

Letter O and Z

To get the benefit of these letters, the name could begin with either O or Z.

Companies with Name Number 7
(source- http://fortune.com/global500/list/)

Company name	Name Number
APPLE	25/7
IBM	7
AMERISOURCEBERGEN	61/7

People with Name Number 7

Power Names	Name Number

Ma Huateng	34/7
Steve Ballmer	43/7
Bernard Arnault	43/7
Bill Gates	25/7

Summing Up -

- **Step 1** - Find the meaning of your day of birth, strengths and weakness
- **Step 2** - Find out the meaning of your power number by adding all the numbers of your birthdate. Pick the career or job or business as per the final number and your interests.
- **Step 3** - Find out your name number values and its meaning. If it's lucky use it as usual. If it's not, consult a professional to bring it on a more harmonious name number.
- **Step 4** - Find out your personal year and what it might bring.
- **Step 5** - Find out your personal day before you start a job or business or new venture.
- **Step 6** - Find out your lucky days and dates to set up meetings or events to bring success.
- **Step 7** - On a daily basis keep your lucky color and solutions with you either use in your clothing or wallet/handbag. Keep a square made of sea green cloth or yellow construction paper and write number 25 on it in sea green color. Write your day of birth of 7, 16 or 25 on it in yellow color (don't worry even if you can't see it). Keep this in your wallet or purse and change it every full moon. If it helps, continue doing it.
- **Bonus -**
- Number 7 people achieve success by hard work and face some issues. They can wear Moonstone for success. Cat's eye and Pearl will also produce good results. If cost is a concern, then follow Step 7.
- The year that is of your lucky number series would be good. This year is 2017 that adds to 1. If it's your lucky number or friendly number, then this year will bring great results too. Also, the year of your age if it's of lucky number series, then it will bring great success. Suppose, you are born on 25/7 and you turned 43/7 in 2017. So this year would

bring remarkable results based on if the number has proved to you lucky or not.

(Do consult a professional number-influencer before you follow any recommendations for the most beneficial results)

"Born on October 26, 1883 (day 26 adds to number 8) in a one room cabin and losing his mother at the age of 9. He started writing at the age of 13 (adds to 4). He went through many trials and tribulations that a number 8 goes through. He ultimately found his passion and achieved the fame for his book "THINK AND GROW RICH". This book is among the top 10 best-selling self-help books of all time. Number 8 takes a lot of time to shine but once there it stays forever."

- Meet Napoleon Hill, American self-help author

Another example of extraordinary success of number 8 is of Chef Gordon Ramsey, born on November 8, 1966 who has received 14 Michelin Stars.

CHAPTER 8 - ALL ABOUT NUMBER 8

Affirmations - "I receive abundance of joy and happiness every day."

Number 8 is the "touch me not Number." Its ruling planet is Saturn. It requires the world's best surgeon to even look at it. This number is the karmic number, and the life it provides is all the result of previous karma. Love it or like it or hate it, you have to take it. You cannot leave it.

It was the quest to make the life of Number 8 better that led me to learn this predictive science.

Number 8 is hard work, struggles, delay and back to square one. This number also represents wealth. For Number 8 to lead a happy and successful life, few changes need to be made.

The success to Number 8 is guaranteed in one sphere, and if you know that, then this number is the king of this space.

Their life is full of unexpected happenings, misfortune, and delays. However, the GOOD NEWS is you can minimize the ill-effect and pick between good or bad choices.

This number gives you results based on past and present deeds. While other numbers give you materialistic success, this number gives you spiritual success, and materialistic success comes as a reward.

A word of caution - This number can produce confusion and indecisiveness.

Characteristics:
They have great mental strength and willpower. This mental power is the key to turning the negative effects into a positive one. This positive outlook will help overcome all problems boldly.

Their early life will be filled with problems either financial or loss of one of parent or health or emotional. But they can come out of it with a victory. They have to be very careful during the years that is of Number 8 series such as 8,17,26, 35, and 44 as it may cause great problems.

They make friends easily with those born on either 1st, 4th, and 8th series and they will be helpful to them.

Day Number 8
Those born on 8th, 17th, and 26th of any given month are Number 8 personalities. The day number is the key to understanding your talents and strengths.

Life Purpose -
Those born on any date of any given month but having the power number 8 are also Number 8 personalities. It's key to find which business or career will bring you success.

Zodiac Ruler -
If your zodiac sign is Capricorn or Aries, you are ruled by Planet Saturn and Number 8. Knowing the ruling planet can help you figure out the solutions to minimize harmful effects. This usually is done by the name change, use of colors, signature style, and few other things.

Name Number -
If the alphabet values in your name add to 8, then you are ruled by Number 8 too.

Specific characteristics:

Day 8 –
This is a great personality where the heart craves for spiritual pursuits and mind craves for materialistic success. They love peaceful and happy life. Their mind is at peace if they are occupied in some social pursuits that benefit the community. Their biggest strength is their willpower.

Day 17 –
Notice how this number has 1 and 7, this helps them either be born in riches or achieve massive wealth and enjoy life. They can go any length to achieve wealth and power. This number is one of the lucky series of Number 8. They do not enjoy the life as they collect money and not like to spend.

Day 26 –
Notice how number 2 and 6 both family members make this up. This life will bring them various tests to fulfill those responsibilities. Often they lose their parents, see lack of personal growth or education in their early life. This makes them strong and helps them achieve wealth and success in the later years of life. They always seem to be aloof and suffer from anxiety.

Various variations of Name Number 8 series
(How to calculate name number is shown in the section titled "Introduction")

As mentioned previously, if the name number adds to 9 series, then you will be under the influence of Number 9 too. Below are the specific characteristics of various variations of Name Number 8.

Name Number 8 - If the name number adds to 8, then success is achieved after a lot of struggle. This will bring great success in religious and spiritual life.

Name Number 17- This name number is a mystic. Someone who has to go a lot of struggle in early life and then achieves success and fame.

Name Number 26 - This name number will bring losses from friends and poverty in a later part of your life. Money making can land you in big trouble too.

Name Number 35 - This name number makes one suffer due to relationships. They seem to earn a lot but then lose a lot too. Be careful of your investments.

Name Number 44 - This number and age will bring you money easily, but there are dangers to life due to accidents.

Name Number 53 - Number 5 here will give them either stability or loss early on in life and Number 3 gets them stability by finding their creative powers. However, if other numbers are lucky, then this result will take place. Else Number 53 makes one very short-tempered.

Lucky Dates -
Those who have the number 8 influence either by way of a day or power number or name number or ruling planet, they can start using their lucky dates.

These dates are series of 1 and 4.
1st, 10th, 19th, 4th, 13th, 22nd, 31st.

Using lucky dates increases chances of success, favorable networking, successful partnerships, and long-lasting positive success.

Friendly Dates -
The dates of 9th will be favorable too in your life. These dates could bring good fortune.

Try to do your important meetings, events, deals and efforts on 27th usually as that is most beneficial.

Unlucky Dates -
Unfortunately, their series is their most unfortunate. Dates 8th, 17th and 26th of any given month should be avoided as these will add to the misery, struggle, difficulties, and failures.

Line of Work -
Their willpower and mental strength helps them rise to high administrative positions. Especially those born on 17th will rise to high positions of justice system such as attorneys, judges, and legal experts.

In fact, Number 8 being responsibility, if you have 8 by way of day and power number or name number, chances are you might rise to take the lead role of a nation.

Number 8 is a teacher and a spiritual guru. These people can work in the mines, hygiene industry, oil and natural gas, arbitrators, spiritual teachers, head of religious institutions and partnerships of these.

Remember using this information can help you decide which areas are suitable for you as per your day number or power number or zodiac number to get name and fame!

Business Partners -
Number 8 people have the very strong will and are hardworking. They sometimes get misunderstood by others. However, it would be wise to do business partnerships with people born under the influence of 1, 4, and 5.

If possible avoid partnerships but if not, then try NOT to partner with people of the series of 6. Experience shows number 15 particularly proves fatal for Number 8 people.

Number 8 people will usually support you in rain or shine. So, keep that in mind too. They make great lifelong trustworthy friends.

Personal Relationships -
Number 8 people thrive if partnered with Number 1, 4 and 8 series. Number 6 could be a good partner too but avoid those born on 15th as a partner.

The power number of people born on day 8 could also be a great partner. Suppose you were born on January 8th, 1956. Add 1+8+21= 12/3. In this case, the power number is 3. If they partner with people of number 3 series, that will prove lucky too.

Their married life is not a happy one. But they should avoid partnerships with Number 2, 7 and 9 as it can be a disaster.

MILLION DOLLAR ADVISE - Equally important is to select a good marriage date but avoid dates of Number 5 series at all cost.

Lucky Colors -
From using your lucky colors in your d cor, personal clothing, a business logo to anything, the possibilities are endless. This is an easy way to get maximum benefit from your lucky numbers by using the relevant lucky colors in your daily life.

Lucky colors for number 8 are various shades of yellow and dark green. They can use blue but in moderation.

Unlucky Colors -
Avoid red, black, brown and pastel shades as it doesn't support the positive vibrations of number 8.

Precious Stones & Metal -
Blue sapphire will bring great fortune and success. It will ensure success in your ventures and relieve you from delays as well sufferings.

Solutions-

If you are facing health issues, use your lucky stone.
If you are facing financial issues, give something in charity on Saturday. If you cannot do this, take out a dollar every saturday for donating and then you can use it buy someone free meal or give it away in charity.
You can also donate every month black sesame seeds oil or 8 tablespoons black sesame seeds to a needy or to an orphanage.
You can keep a coin made of dark green cloth or yellow construction paper and write your birth day number of 8, 17 or 26 on it in dark green color. Do not worry if you cannot see it. Keep this in your wallet or purse and change it every full moon. If it helps continue doing it.
Avoid eating meat on Saturday or dates of 8, 17, and 26.
For overall benefits, meditate while holding 1 tablespoon white rice in your hand and then letting rice flow in running water of your kitchen sink. Do this every Saturday.

Wear your lucky colors on a daily basis.
Your marriage is usually delayed. To avoid that, use solutions of number 3 or keep a small piece of silver with you all times.

IMPORTANT THING TO REMEMBER:

These English alphabets have been given the value of number 8:

Letter F and P

To get the benefit of these letters, the name should begin with either F or P.

MOST IMPORTANT TIP:

Number 8 can change the course of destiny by changing the name, signature, using the lucky colors of the destiny number or zodiac ruler. However, experience shows that only the name change that adds to Number 5 benefits them.

This is the key to enhancing the benefits of any other number in your date of birth too!

Companies with Name Number 8
(source- http://fortune.com/global500/list/)

Company name	Name Number
EXXON MOBIL	44/8
CVS HEALTH	35/8
FANNIE MAE	35/8
RENAULT	26/8
FACEBOOK	35/8

People with Name Number 8

Power Names	Name Number

LEE SHAU KEE	35/8
LARRY PAGE	26/8
AMANCIO ORTEGA	44/8

Now see the **NUMBERS** of important events in **NAPOLEON HILL's** life:
Example:
Name Number = NAPOLEON HILL =8
Book Name Number= THINK AND GROW RICH=2
Date of Birth = OCTOBER 26,1883
DAY NUMBER = 26/8
POWER NUMBER = 2(10+26+1883)
ZODIAC SIGN = SCORPIO
RULING PLANET = MARS, NUMBER=9

MY PREDICTIONS:
8 & 9 are very unlucky together and will see the influence of 3 and 4 causing harm too. In this case, NUMBER 2 is very lucky. Napoleon Hill's name number is in his unlucky number series and that's why numerology insists on name alignment.

Napoleon Hill's lucky number 2. Number 9 could go either way.
Napoleon Hill's unlucky numbers are 3,4, and 8

Born on October 26, 1883, his life will have strong influence of 8 (day 26/8), 2(10+26+1883=11/2) and his zodiac ruling planet of Scorpio, ruling number 9. Although number 8 could go any way but 2 and 9 will bring some positive life changing results.

1883 (adds 2)- He was born in Virginia

1907 (adds 8)- He founded Acree Hill Lumber Company which later went into BANKRUPTCY

1908 (adds to 9) - Andrew Carnegie introduced him to a huge opportunity by asking to organize the world's first philosophy of personal achievement

1910 (adds to 2)- Napoleon Hill married to Florence Elizabeth Horner.

Later he embarked on other business ventures including Betsy Ross Candy Shop, George Washington Institute of Advertising, personal magazines including Hill's Golden Rule, Napoleon Hill's magazine and Intra-Wall Correspondence School but all failed.

1912 (adds to 4)- He declared BANKRUPTCY for his Automobile College of Washington

1919 (adds to 2)- He published Hill's Golden Rules Magazine.

1921 (adds to 4)- He published Napoleon Hill's Magazine.

1928 (adds to 2)-Napoleon Hill moved to Philadelphia and released his successful work, "The Law of Success."

1930 (adds to 4)- Napoleon Hill published his work The Magic Ladder to Success, which didn't quite bring success.

1933 (adds to 5)- He acted as the Presidential Advisor to the President Franklin D. Roosevelt

1937 (adds to 2)- This number 2 year brought his all-time success with the best-selling book titled **"Think & Grow Rich"**

1939 (adds to 4)- Napoleon Hill published "How to Sell Your Way Through Life."

1941 (adds to 6)- He published his 17 volumes study course titled "Mental Dynamite."

1942 (adds to 7)- Napoleon Hill's program titled Mental Dynamite was discontinued due to World War II

1945 (adds to 1)- Napoleon Hill's published his work titled "The Master Key to Riches."

1952 (adds to 8)- Napoleon Hill teaches his philosophy on "Science of Success"

1953 (adds to 9)- Napoleon Hill published his work titled "How to Raise Your Own Salary."

1959 (adds to 6)- Hill published another work titled "Success Through a Positive Mental Attitude."

1961 (adds to 8)- Napoleon Hill published another work titled "PMA Science of Success Course."

This is a perfect example of how ruling numbers were his best years and changed the course of his life. It's all about NUMBERS.

Summing Up -

- **Step 1** - Find the meaning of your day of birth, strengths and weakness
- **Step 2** - Find out the meaning of your power number by adding all the numbers of your birthdate. Pick the career or job or business as per the final number and your interests.
- **Step 3** - Find out your name number values and its meaning. If it's lucky use it as usual. If it's not, consult a professional to bring it on a more harmonious name number.
- **Step 4** - Find out your personal year and what it might bring.
- **Step 5** - Find out your personal day before you start a job or business or new venture.
- **Step 6** - Find out your lucky days and dates to set up meetings or events to bring success.
- **Step 7** - On a daily basis keep your lucky color and solutions with you. Keep a coin made of dark green cloth or yellow construction paper and write your birth day number of 8, 17 or 26 on it in dark green color. Do not worry if you cannot see it. Keep this in your wallet or purse and change it every full moon. If it helps continue doing it.
- **Bonus** -
- Number 8 people achieve success after struggles but their success is unmatched by any other number. You cannot bring them down easily. So, trust your instincts.
- The year that is of your lucky number series would be good. This year is 2017 that adds to 1. If it's your lucky number or friendly number,

then this year will bring great results too. Also, the year of your age if it's of lucky number series, then it will bring great success. Suppose, you are born on 26/8 and you turned 44/8 in 2017. So, this year would bring remarkable results based on if the number has proved to you lucky or not.

(Do consult a professional number-influencer before you follow any recommendations for the most beneficial results)

"Born on July 18, 1918, (number 18 adds to 9), he was a South African anti-apartheid revolutionary leader, philanthropist, political leader and also served as President of South Africa. Number 9 is the number of humanitarian leaders as well social activist.

- Meet NELSON MANDELA

Another example of extraordinary success is of the French chef, Jean Sulpice, born on July 27, 1978 (27 adds to 9), who is known for being the youngest French chef to have ever received a Michelin Star at the age of 26!

CHAPTER 9 - ALL ABOUT NUMBER 9

Nine is a builder, arbitrator and the "BIG DADDY" of the humanitarian causes as well fire industry. Fiery planet Mars rules number 9 personalities. They have the power of the fire, the passion, and the willpower to turn any obstacle around. They either shine in social areas or in an industry where fire rules such as food industry, hotel, restaurants, iron industry, manufacturing of metal and its products.

Number 9 is a fighter, and they overcome every struggle and come back every time just like "PHOENIX."

Day Number 9 -
Those born on 9th, 18th, and 27th of any given month are Number 9 personalities. The day number is the key to understanding your talents and strengths.

Life Purpose -
Those born on any date of any given month but having the power number 9 are also Number 9 personalities. It's key to find which business or career will bring you success.

Zodiac Ruler -
If your zodiac sign is Aries or Scorpio, you are ruled by Planet Mars and Number 9. Knowing the ruling planet can help you either maximize the beneficial results of your lucky number or minimize the harmful results of unlucky number influence. This usually is done by the name change.

Name Number -
If the alphabet values in your name add to 9, then you are ruled by Number 9 too.

Characteristics -
Number 9 people are fighters as life doesn't deliver greatness to them without struggles. Their intelligence is the key as they are very sharp and some of them join an army and shine there. Their success comes by doing something that enriches the life of the community.

However, you do not want to fight back with them as they will get back to you no matter what. The key is to know how to balance their fiery nature with the diplomacy and play as per the situation and opponents.

Remember the day number 9 gives a boost to the influence of other numbers in your date of birth.

Number 9 people in the personal life are faced with a lot of struggles, delays, and problems. However, no matter what, number 9 works hard and come back with a bang!!

Their success mantra is to invest in doing good for the society. Do something that benefits the social cause, and they get rewarded. They always experience struggles especially early life. Success comes back to them once they overcome the initial challenges.

Remember Number 9 is fire, the power and helps you get the energy and courage to do things in action and not just think.

Specific Characteristics:

Day Number 9 –
Number 9 born are very ambitious and have high dreams. They can make things happen but need to live by high ideals.

Day Number 18 –
This number 9 influences number 1, and that makes them an ambitious leader. With the influence of karmic number 8, they seem to get confused with the pull towards spiritual side too. This causes misunderstandings in their relationships too. They should meditate to keep their mental energy on the positive side and not make rash decisions.

Day Number 27 –
This Number 9 will never do wrong to others and always find success. You could call them peacemakers and great diplomats.

VARIOUS VARIATIONS OF NAME NUMBER 9 SERIES
(How to calculate name number is shown in the section titled "Introduction")

As mentioned previously, if the name number adds to 9 series, then you will be under the influence of Number 9 too. Below are the specific characteristics of various variations of Name Number 9.

Name Number 9 - This is a wise number and imparts wisdom and strength to face the struggles and bring success.

Name Number 18 - This number is not a materialistic number. This belongs to sages, preachers and religious heads who renounce the world to seek divinity.

Name Number 27 - This name number brings clarity of visions, mind, and purpose of life. This is a lucky name number to have as they success in social service and brings charisma.

Name Number 36 - This name number is a strange one though very fortunate to have. This name number can raise even one from rags to riches but only if they leave their birthplace and travel far. They seem to have an unstable family life.

Name Number 45 - This is another lucky name number to have in the Number 9 series. They are great communicators, hardworking, and seem to have a successful life. However, watch out for health problems.

Name Number 54 - Notice how it has 5 and 4. This number brings success after failures. However, the desire to have quick success can lead them to troubles. So remember to look at the long-term success.

Lucky Dates -
Those who have the number 9 influence either by way of a day or power number or name number, they can start using their lucky dates.

These dates are series of 3, 5, 6 and 9.
3rd, 21st, 6th, 15th, 24th, 5th, 14th, 23rd, 27th, and 30th.
Notice that I am not recommending either 12th, 9th and 18th even though it's in their lucky dates series because experience shows it doesn't benefit them.

Using lucky dates increases chances of success, favorable networking, successful partnerships, and long-lasting positive results.

Try to do your important meetings, events, deals and efforts on 27th usually as that is most beneficial in your number 9 series.

Friendly Dates -
The dates of 1st and 19th will be favorable too in your life. The changes would be beneficial as well unpredictable.

Unlucky Dates -

Dates 2th, 11th, 20th and 29th of any given month should be avoided as these will add to the misery, struggle, difficulties, and failures.

Line of Work -
Their mental strength helps them remain calm and use this power wisely. They are fond of research, thrive in the areas of medicine, engineering, real estate, iron and steel, construction, solar powered areas, food industry and unrevealing the divine mystic secrets

Remember using this information can help you decide which areas are suitable for you as per your day number or power number to get name and fame!

Business Partners -
Number 9 people are very strong minded and hardworking. They believe in working hard and don't play to fool others! However, it would be wise to do business partnerships with people born under the influence of 3,5,6 and 9 only.

If possible avoid partnerships but if not, then try to partner with people of the number series of 3,5, and 6.

Number 8 people will usually support you in rain or shine. So, keep that in mind too.

LIGHTBULB: This is where numerology is very helpful as a number-influencer can advise on the business prospect, future of your business and also which line of work/business will be fortunate based on your day, power, and name number. Not to forget the zodiac number and its influence too.

Personal Relationships -
Just imagine 2 strong people together just like two Number 9 can be a disaster. So, in a personal relationship, you might be happy if married to people from number 3 and 6 series.

However, I do not recommend number 5 as this number rules mind, and your relationships need to be supportive not overwhelming.

Lucky Colors -
From using your lucky colors in your d cor, personal clothing, a business logo to anything, the possibilities are endless. This is an easy way to get maximum benefit from your lucky numbers by using the relevant lucky colors in your daily life.

Lucky colors for number 9 are dark shades of red and blue.

Unlucky Colors -
Avoid white and shades of green as it doesn't support the positive aura of number 9.

Precious Stones & Metal -
Coral will be good from a health perspective and can be worn in a gold or copper ring or pendant in the ring finger on Tuesday.

Solutions-
If you are facing health issues, use your lucky stone.
If you are facing financial issues, give something in charity on Tuesday.
You can also donate every month split red lentils to a needy or to an orphanage.
You can keep a coin made of red cloth or red construction paper and write your birth day number of 9, 18 or 27 on it in red color. Do not worry if you cannot see it. Keep this in your wallet or purse and change it every full moon. If it helps continue doing it.
Avoid eating meat on Tuesday or dates of 9, 18 and 27.
For overall benefits, meditate while holding red flowers in your hand and then letting flowers flow in running water of your sink. Do this every Tuesday.
Wear your lucky colors on a daily basis.
Set up important meetings or interview on your lucky days or dates.

IMPORTANT THING TO REMEMBER -
None of the English alphabets have been given the value of number 9 as it's believed to be the most divine number and any number added or multiplied by number 9 retains its identity.

This is the key to enhancing the benefits of any other number in your date of birth too!

Companies with Name Number 9
(source- http://fortune.com/global500/list/)

Company name	Name Number

State Grid	27/9
AT&T	9
Aeon	18/9
Exor Group	45/9
Ford Motor	45/9
Intel	18/9
Costco	27/9

People with Name Number 9

Power Names	Name Number
Maria Franca Fissolo	54/9

Summing Up -

- **Step 1** - Find the meaning of your day of birth, strengths and weakness
- **Step 2** - Find out the meaning of your power number by adding all the numbers of your birthdate. Pick the career or job or business as per the final number and your interests.
- **Step 3** - Find out your name number values and its meanings. If it's lucky use it as usual. If it's not, consult a professional to bring it on a more harmonious name number.
- **Step 4** - Find out your personal year and what it might bring.
- **Step 5** - Find out your personal day before you start a job or business or new venture.
- **Step 6** - Find out your lucky days and dates to set up meetings or events to bring success.
- **Step 7** - On a daily basis keep your lucky color and solutions with you. Either in your clothing or wallet/handbag or take a circle shape of red cloth or construction paper and write your day number 9,18 or 27 on it in red color (don't worry even if you can't see it) and put it in your wallet/handbag.
- **Bonus** - Number 9 people are lucky and can face some health issues. They can wear Coral for success. If cost is a concern, then follow Step 7.

(Do consult a professional number-influencer before you follow any recommendations for the most beneficial results)

Let's explain it with **an example.** I am using a fictitious name of John Mayers born on August 27, 1968.

Step 1- Find out your talents, strengths and weakness for number 9 and date 27.

Step 2- Find out your purpose by adding your date of birth. Find its meaning. In this example, it adds to 8+27+1968=41/5. Find the business or profession for number 5. Also see the business or profession for number 9. Decide where your interests lie.

Step 3- Next add the name numbers values to find the final number and its meaning. In this case, John Mayers adds to 34/7 (J=1, O=7, H=5, N=5 = 18; M=4, A=1, Y=1, E=5, R=2, S=3= 16; John (18) + Mayer (16)=34/7)

Step 4- Find your personal year to see how this year will be for you. In this case, let's find out- Add birthday+birth month+current year; 27+8+2017=27/9.

So, this year is number 9 and find out the meaning of number 9. (given in the introduction section)

Step 5 - Next find out the personal day you want to start a new business or register or go for interview. Let's assume that John wants to start his business on December 10, 2017. Is that day lucky or good? Let's find out- add your birth day+birth month + current day+current month+current year. So 27+8+10+12+2017=4. So, December 10th is personal day 4 for John. Find its meaning to see if it's lucky to start or register your new business or venture.

Step 6- Use your lucky days and lucky dates to set up important event or meetings on a regular basis.

Step 7- If the current year is no favorable and you are facing challenges, then use the lucky colors, lucky solutions and cures on a daily basis.

Bonus- Consult a professional for getting your name number aligned on a lucky vibration and for few changes in your signature patterns.

BONUS- I am sharing here the meanings of the first letter of the name and how it impacts your overall personality.

First name Initials and Their Meanings:

"A" alphabet is number 1 and symbolizes the attribute of confidence, bold and courageous.

People with the first letter of A are confident, bold, creators, innovators, leaders, and visionaries. However, they can be critical of others and arrogant.

"B" alphabet is number 2 and symbolizes the duality. People with the first letter of B are good for partnerships, sympathetic, warm, and are supportive. However, they can be greedy and strong opinionated.

"C" alphabet is number 3 and symbolizes creativity, curiosity, and charisma. People with the first letter of C are optimistic, charming, communicators and thrive with inspiration. However, they can be empathetic and careless.

"D" alphabet is number 4 and symbolizes rules, regulation, and organization. People with alphabet D are hardworking and often successful in business or wealth management. However, they are not adventurous, risk takers and do not like to change which sometimes proves detrimental.

"E" alphabet is number 5 and symbolizes traveler and carefree personality. People with alphabet E are highly intuitive, imaginative, flexible and easily accept change. However, they are very opinionated, unreliable, and stubborn.

"F" alphabet is number 6 and symbolizes easy going, loving and caring personalities. People with alphabet F are responsible, family-orientated, artistic and nature lovers. However, being demanding they are hard to themselves and if don't meet the expectations, then feel pity for themselves.

"G" alphabet is number 7 and symbolizes mystical, spiritual and religious personalities. People with alphabet G are creative, highly intuitive, intelligent, imaginative, and truth seekers. However, being inquisitive, they tend to enjoy loneliness, judge others, and often ignore near and dear ones around them. They need to listen to their well-wishers.

"H" alphabet is the number 8 and symbolizes wealth, power, wisdom, and business acumen. People with H alphabet have a vision, are strong-willed, have the ability to create wealth and power for themselves, and are natural leaders. However, they are short-tempered, do not appreciate others easily, ignore minor details, lack practicality and are greedy for power.

"I" is the number 9 and symbolizes compassionate personalities who thrive on charity, are dependable, make great peace makers, diplomats, and are fighters for the social cause. People with I alphabet are humanitarians, thought leaders, and intelligent. However, they miss the realistic picture of their vision, fail to take others help, and friends turn out to be their worst enemies.

"J" is the number 1 and symbolizes powerful, charismatic, truthful, and hardworking personalities. People with J alphabet can be multi-talented and can have many professions as they are self-starters, and conscientious. They thrive best when they pursue a leadership role, are motivators and visionaries that help the humanitarian causes as they are blessed with intuition and divine innate powers that provide them direction in life. However, being multi-talented it gets hard to decide on one aspect of career and that makes them a bouncy ball that keeps switching from one career to others. Their intuition is their power.

"K" is the number 2 and symbolizes someone who can go to any length to get things done. People with K alphabet need to learn to balance as they are strong-willed but are great friends, arbitrators, and caretakers. However, one needs to understand them and win their trust first and that at times can be difficult and this makes them dissatisfied with life and life situations.

"L" is the number 3 and symbolizes hard worker, communicator, and a creator. People with L alphabet are friendly, sociable and great inspiration to others. A person with the initial L is most often a charitable, loving, enjoyable, and friendly person.

As a matter of fact, they are best for the professions that involve communications of any kinds such as TV, media, journalism, teaching, etc. However, they can sometimes be careless and thus accident prone.

"M" is the number 4 and symbolizes authentic, stability, spirituality, and organized personality. People with M alphabet are traditional, conservative and live by rules of high ethics. This makes them dependable, knowledgeable and helps them earn wealth too. However, they hate to change and that can be difficult at times. They like to know the plan and can't just jump impromptu into any plan!

"N" is the number 5 and symbolizes imaginative, and fun-loving personality. People with N alphabet are very active, love to travel, enjoy extravagance, unpredictable, unconventional, and are very opportunistic. However, they are very persuasive and are naturally inquisitive. They do not like to follow the conventional path and sometimes disposed to enmity and jealousy.

"O" is the number 6 and one of the most influential, lucky, and powerful alphabet along with A, J, M, and S. It symbolizes someone who achieves power through his loving and nurturing nature. People with O alphabet are adventurers, torchbearers, and visionaries who have great intuitive powers. They have a charismatic personality.

However, they fight for their ideals, beliefs, and for the right and this gets them in trouble at times. They are a fair and strong believer of justice.

"P" is the number 7 and symbolizes intuition, power, and spirituality. People with P alphabet have a great desire to learn and are blessed with abilities that will help them in becoming a great mentor or guru in any field. They don't associate with everyone but keep their natural instincts groomed and connect when they feel connected.

However, with their aloofness, they keep their inner feelings to themselves and don't share. This can be misunderstood by others as being selfish or careless. They should try to balance their mysticism and introvert nature.

"Q" is the number 8 and symbolizes power, wealth, and stability. People with Q alphabet have a great deal of courage, integrity, willpower and always work for the growth of humanity. That is where they thrive professionally too! Amazingly they are blessed with divine patience, loyalty, and inner guide that helps them achieve their goal.
However, a Q person can be often too ignorant about his surroundings and self-absorbed.

"R" is the number 9 and symbolizes tolerance, wisdom, diplomat, compassion, intuition, and educator. People with R alphabet have the love for family, friends, and can be very creative. They enjoy comfortable and luxurious life.

Their strength is their idealism and compassion. This could be very well a rewarding career for them if done with the intention of serving others. However, a BIG warning do not let others take you for granted or don't let yourself to become martyrs! It's good to speak up rather than hold inside and become short-tempered, tensed, and stressed.

"S" is the number 1 and symbolizes one of the most powerful letters along with A, J, M, and O. People with "S" alphabet lead, guide, and have the ability to get things done. Being number 1, they are very ambitious, self-confident, and have always new ideas to go for. They could be a good partner in personal and professional relationships as they are loyal, supportive, and intelligent.

However, living with S could be overwhelming as they do not like to play second fiddle, they get impulsive if not acknowledged, and also their desire to lead could let the other partner feel like a doormat and a martyr. As I say no 2 swords fit together, NEVER should 2 people with Number 1 stay together. It's like placing 2 SUN on the same horizon. Guess what will happen?

"T" is the number 2 and symbolizes balance, maturity, harmony, and peacemaker. People with T alphabet make great diplomats, mediator, and achieve great success by playing a supportive role to the leadership, being their shadow, bringing their loyalty, peace-making skills, and nurturing nature.

This is the profession where they can achieve amazing success, by playing the second fiddle as no leader can thrive if they don't have a strong team, support, and stable partner. 2 is that partner be it in professional life or personal relationships. However, if Number T is ignored, not acknowledged, and made aware of the developments about personal or professional ideas, plans, or changes, then they can revolt. Now take your pick. Do you want to lose the most loyal and efficient partner or do you want to share the plans? They always try to bring peace and harmony in the toughest situations.

They are very emotional just like a child, all they need is the feeling of belonging and trust. They get easily influenced by others opinions and can become indecisive.

"**U**" is the number 3 and symbolizes a social, charming, entertaining and lucky person. Number 3 represents Jupiter, the planet of luxury, beauty, and intellect. So are the People with U alphabet. They can always turn any simple thing into a work of art. They can thrive in the areas of music, painting, designing, culinary arts, drama and such. They like to be appreciated, admired, Loved and acknowledged. This gets sometimes hard for others in their environment. They have the strong intuitive ability but they need to meditate to groom. They tend to ignore their own inner guidance system and often get into hurtful emotional or professional relationships.

However, as they enjoy luxury they often get greedy, selfish and hard to please. They need to learn to live within their means.

"**V**" is the number 4 and symbolizes someone who can be your hidden enemy and ready to sting if things do not go their way, otherwise they are efficient and hardworking. Their core nature is selfish and if they overcome that, then they are organized, practical, dependable, and detail oriented.

However, they can be ruthless and often don't show their true motive and are ready to take their action when they see the moment is right.

"**W**" is number 5 and symbolizes artistic, creative, freedom, and someone who loves to live on their own terms. People with W alphabet don't like routine life, they always want change, they can't be held onto one idea, place or situations in life for long as it is suffocating for them. However, they need to watch their tendencies of over-indulgence, rash decision making, and impulsiveness. Their own nature is their biggest weakness. They get bored easily, always want change else they feel trapped be it personal or professional relationships.

They often make mistakes by taking rash decisions.

"**X**" is the number 6 and symbolizes caring, loving, sensual personality. People with X alphabet always want love, stability, comforts, and warmth. This nature makes them great yoga instructor, trainer, parent, and healer.

However, their strong personality makes them anxious, selfish, and highly opinionated. As they love comforts, they do not like to be rushed or judged. For comforts, they will trade their loyalty!

"Y" is the number 7 and symbolizes great intuitive, spiritual and intelligent personalities. Their true nature is of seeking, finding out and exposing the truth. They are very observant and can easily judge the situations based on facts or opinions.

However, given their judgmental and introspective personality, they can get swayed from their own path if use their inner powers for harming others. They can be great lawyers, judges, arbitrators, parents, and teachers.

"Z" is the number 8 and symbolizes hope, peace, practical, and dependable personality. People with Z alphabet could be a boss, manager, leader, and they are very practical when it comes to money, business, and power.

Due to their own nature, they make great business owners, high achievers, and movers & shakers. They are strong-willed and courageous. They seem to accumulate a lot of wealth in their life. They go for what they believe in.

However, they are so demanding that not everybody can keep up with their speed or expectations and they often act hastily.

DISCLAIMER

Although the author and publisher have made every effort to ensure that the information in this book was correct at press time, the author and publisher do not assume and hereby disclaim any liability to any party for any loss, damage, or disruption caused by errors or omissions, whether such errors or omissions result from negligence, accident, or any other cause.

Further, this book is not intended as a substitute for the medical advice of physicians or other service professionals pertaining to mind, body or spiritual healing. The reader should regularly consult a certified professional in matters relating to his/her emotional, financial, physical and overall health and particularly with respect to any symptoms that may require diagnosis or medical or professional attention.

Conclusion:

The numerology could best be explained as something that can be used in everyday life as a predictive tool for your day and year, so you can plan accordingly. I often say it's like a weather channel that predicts your hours, day, weeks and month so you can plan and prepare yourself for the upcoming weather.

This predictive science is very accurate and using it would help you to be prepared for the coming years that could be very helpful in preparing to face it. What if you know that the next year will be harsh on you in terms of health or job or relationship?

That does not mean that you can avoid it just like weather predictions, you cannot but you can prepare yourself, for sure. Each number has either a positive effect or a negative effect. When it's positive, you experience success, progress, name and fame. When it's negative, you go through struggles, delays, failures and trials.

Although one cannot change that but NUMBER-SCIENCE enhances the positive effects and minimizes the negative effects by way of solutions. I have given to you the 7 Steps to Creating Success with NUMBERS.

BRINGING IT ALL TOGETHER

Number 1 - These people are ruled by planet Sun. They should begin their work on important dates of 1 and 4 series and avoid 8 series. Ruby stone in gold and yellow color is great for them.

Number 2 - These people are ruled by planet Moon. They should do their important tasks on the dates of 1 and 7 series. Avoid number 2 and 8 series. The light green color, silver, Pearl and moonstone would be very favorable.

Number 3 - These people are ruled by planet Jupiter. They should do their important meetings on dates of number 3 series. They should avoid number 6 series dates. Number 1,2 and 3 series will be supportive. The orange tones and Amethyst should be used for more fortune.

Number 4 - These people are ruled by strong mental power and thus meditation as well yoga would be great. They are ruled by planet Uranus. Their important dates are mostly of 1number 1 series. The number 2 and 4 will be supportive. The should use light blue as well yellow tones on a regular basis. Hessonite would be great for their overall success.

Number 5 - These people are ruled by planet Mercury. They should do important deals on dates of 5 and 9 series. They find support from 1,4,5 and 9. Grey color and Diamonds should be used on a daily basis.

Number 6 - These people are ruled by planet Venus. They should begin their important things on 6 and 9 series. Avoid number 3 and 5 series. Darker shades of green, blue and red along with Emerald should be used.

Number 7 - These people are ruled by planet Neptune. Their lucky dates are 25, and 2 number series. Dates of other number 7 and 8 series should be avoided. Number 1 and 4 are supportive too. Lighter shades of white as well yellow is great for them. Pearls and Cat's eye should be used.

Number 8 - These people are ruled by planet Saturn. Dates of 1, 10 and 19th are helpful. They should avoid all number 8 series. THEY SHOULD NOT BEGIN IMPORTANT THINGS ON NUMBER 6 SERIES. Number 5 is the ONLY number that seems to help them get better life and success. Thus, you should follow number 5 suggestions.

Number 9 - These people are ruled by planet Mars. Number 5, 6 and 9 series are great for you. Avoid number 2 dates. Red color and Coral would be great for you.

If you have any questions, get in touch with me on my social handle as well as on my website.

http://www.invinciblepassiontalkshow.com/about-us/

https://twitter.com/1JayaMK

https://www.instagram.com/jayamkinvincble/

https://www.facebook.com/InvinciblePassionTalkshow/

https://www.facebook.com/jaya.m.karamchandani

Email: Invinciblepassiontalkshow@gmail.com

CPSIA information can be obtained
at www.ICGtesting.com
Printed in the USA
LVHW020053121021
700150LV00010BA/1568